Jen,

Thank you for the kind comment. Hopefully, the book will bring back good memories

Quetico-Superior

A Short History
And Other Stories

By

Mack Van Allen

First Published November 19, 2019

Copy Number:

Book cover design completed by David Hanks

Front book cover photograph taken by Scott Popoff

Back book cover photograph taken by Matthew Turton

ISBN (Print Edition): 978-1-54399-817-7

ISBN (eBook Edition): 978-1-54399-818-4

To my wife and companion
Patricia Drake
and
my son
Eric Van Allen
Safe travels in the
canoe country

That's the wild for you – it's got its dangers, which is part of the beauty.

Lonesome Dove

TABLE OF CONTENTS

A HISTORY

In 1970, I began a special relationship with an untrammeled wilderness located in northeastern Minnesota and north-western Ontario. The Minnesota part of this adjoined wilderness was, at the time, called the Boundary Waters Canoe Area (BWCA), and its Canadian counterpart is Quetico Provincial Park. Together the two areas comprise about nearly 2,000 interconnected lakes spread over 2 million acres. The Quetico-Superior wilderness, as it is sometimes referred to, is a perfect setting for wilderness canoe travel.

That year my friend, Jim Rowley, and I organized our first high school canoe trip in Centerville, Ohio, a venture that would continue over the next twenty-five years. The previous year the Minnesota portion of the canoe country became embroiled in a controversy that threatened the pristine nature of this wilderness. The dispute began when a New York businessman, George W. St. Clair, declared his intentions to exercise mining exploration rights that he claimed to own in the BWCA. St. Clair's action was the beginning salvo in a struggle that would span the next ten years and ultimately determine the future protection accorded to this pristine canoe country.

I traveled annually in the canoe country through all of this. Here and there, I would pick up pieces of the ongoing controversy, but I never felt that I had assembled a comprehensive understanding of this struggle.

Even by 1978, when the United States Congress passed and President Carter signed the *Boundary Waters Canoe*

Area Wilderness Act bringing an end to this rancorous affair, much of the controversy remained confusing. Therefore, during the summer of 1979, I took it upon myself to find out what happened, and, more importantly, how and why it happened. The role of journalist I assumed, although with much naiveté about the ease of the task upon which I was embarking.

In the spring of 1979, I wrote to Bob Franklin, Minneapolis Tribune's city editor. As a result, Dean Rebuffoni, a reporter who had covered various aspects of the controversy, contacted me. Dean was both helpful and generous with his time, allowing me access to the Tribune's morgue containing the paper's extensive coverage of this controversy. My week long examination of the newspaper's articles allowed me to construct a timeline of events and identify the principal players in this wilderness drama.

Following my stay in Minneapolis, I traveled to Duluth and Ely, Minnesota; Atikokan and Toronto, Ontario; and finally to Washington, DC. A parallel controversy involving Quetico Provincial Park had emerged in Canadian shortly after St. Clair's assertion of his mining claims in the BWCA. I conducted interviews with a number of the principal players in this controversy, and examined official government documents and transcripts, and advocacy group publications.

What sprang from my inquiry were the details of a ten year fight that had consumed the politics in two countries, leaving in its wake a tired and embittered group of local residents and an equally tired but mostly satisfied group of wilderness advocates. It was, indeed, a battle of epic dimensions, which deserves a major place in the annals of the twentieth century wilderness wars.

Before telling this story, I must recount two conversations that are as fresh in my memory as if they had happened yesterday. The first was with a Minnesota attorney named Chuck Dayton. As we talked in his downtown Minneapolis office during the summer of 1979, Dayton patiently answered questions that he had no doubt addressed many times before. Behind him on the wall hung a photograph of a canoe floating serenely on a pristine, wilderness lake. His speech was slow and deliberate as he reconstructed from memory the intricate and exhausting details of the ten year struggle to save this wilderness. Lengthy court fights, frustrating bureaucratic appeals and a wrenching legislative effort which had ended in victory the previous year were succinctly reviewed in less than an hour by this young attorney. Dayton at one point characterized his eight year involvement in the wilderness fight as being only a small, though significant, part of "a hundred years' war." He had recently returned from Washington D.C. where he had again argued in federal court in defense of his beloved wilderness. As I listened attentively, I looked across a broad, wooden desk at a man worn but still resolute in his commitment to a struggle that he had surely hoped would have ended the previous year when Congress had acted. Even so, his words were those of a man of conviction who had come to love this wilderness as a boy, and who now found himself, through both circumstance and choice, cast as one of its arch champions. His meaning was clear and without doubt: a course had been struck and there was no question as to its rightness.

Several weeks later, I again sat listening to the words of certitude and conviction. This time, however, I was in Ely, Minnesota, and the speaker had an altogether different take on this whole affair. Frank Salerno, a local businessman and a member of the group pressing the court challenge to which Dayton had just responded, spoke of himself and his friends, of a fiercely independent way of life, of promises made and broken, and, most bitterly, of the political expediency of a bargain, which had leached from the people in this small community the very dignity that they held most dear. He, too, was speaking of the wilderness struggle, but for him its meaning was starkly different, and its outcome was painfully devastating. As he spoke his voice cracked and trembled, barely hiding a deeply felt hurt. Like Dayton, he was a proud man and the rightness of his cause was beyond question.

Of course, the wilderness of which both Dayton and Salerno spoke is the Boundary Waters Canoe Area Wilderness. And for years this canoe country wilderness and its Canadian counterpart have been one of the fulcrums upon which twentieth century society has balanced its relentless drive to develop and produce against its incumbent, though often ignored, responsibility to preserve.

The Crucial Years

The character and history of the Quetico-Superior region has been largely defined by its glacially formed landscape, the native people who lived on its lakes before European intrusion, and the earliest Europeans to travel through this part of North America in search of furs. The last glacial movement 10,000 years ago left behind a scoured and rugged landscape full of pockets of varying size and depth in the hard granite and gabbros rock. As the ice melted, the pockets filled with water, creating the lakes that give this region its defining character. Following years of slow ecological succession, the land again become habitable, dominated by a variety of coniferous tree species, life sustaining patches of wild rice and sugar producing maple trees, and a bountiful supply of fish and fur bearing animals.

The first occupants of this land were native people well adapted to this lake land environment. Today in America their indigenous reference is Native American, and they are commonly called Chippewa; officially designated in Canada as a First Nation, they are commonly referred to as Ojibwa. Essentially they were the same people, members of a culturally related group called the Anishinaabe.

In the Quetico-Superior region, these people lived in this lake land habitat in family groups, gathering together twice yearly to tap the maple trees in the spring and harvest the wild rice in the fall. The native people who occupied the

Quetico-Superior region lived a simple existence, taking from the land and water the food they required for bodily sustenance and the forest materials and animal furs they needed for shelter and clothing so essential to survival in the harsh winters in this region.

It was the furs that first sparked the European interest in this abundant land. In the 1730's, following the exploration of Jacques de Noyon (1688) and Sieur de la Verendryre (1731), a fur trading industry began which lasted close to 100 years. The Quetico-Superior region lay at the heart of a water route which ran west and south from Montreal and Hudson Bay to Canada's northwest lakes – Athabasca, Great Slave and Great Bear. This 3,000 mile commercial waterway was both shop and home for the voyageurs, the brawny laborers of French descent who traveled the vast northern wilderness in their company's service. They were a hardy lot. The tales of their physical exploits, the lyrics of their lively, and sometimes hard to believe, *chansons*, and the canoe routes they left behind are all part of the region's romantic legacy. Yet, no matter how we now idealize these North Country frontiersmen, the fact remains that their coming was inspired by what Thoreau so aptly called man's "want of enterprise." And profit would continue to be the main motive for human involvement in the Quetico-Superior region well into the twentieth century.

Following the French and Indian War that resulted in the cession of French Canada to England, British and American companies replaced the French as the main suppliers of North American furs to Europe. In 1821, the North West Company, the sole remaining French fur trader in the Quetico-Superior region, merged with the Hudson Bay Company and suspended most of its activities in the canoe country. This wilderness attracted little commercial interest for the next fifty years. Then, in 1870, the Quetico was again crossed via the Dawson Route in the great trek west to save Rupert's Land – Canada's vast, unpopulated lands west of Ontario – from stinging bludgeon of America's Manifest Destiny. These people, however, were transients, not resource exploiters. But the exploiters' time was not far off.

As North America's wilderness frontier gradually yielded to civilization's taming hand, and heavy industry in the East and Midwest replaced the small, less efficient manufacturing system of a Pre-Civil War period, the demand for natural resources increased rapidly. Northern Minnesota became a principal supplier of the raw material necessary to fuel this industrial transformation. The iron-rich Mesabi and Vermilion Ranges and the dense, coniferous forests covering the northern part of the state drew ambitious entrepreneurs who were determined to make their fortunes from what God and nature had provided for the taking. In the 1880's, commercial logging started in earnest in the Quetico-Superior region. There was enough timber for all and the supply seemed inexhaustible.

By the turn of the century, however, the State realized the devastating implications of uncontrolled timber harvesting, and it interceded on the forest's behalf. In 1902, based on a recommendation by its own chief fire warden Christopher C. Andrews, Minnesota established its first forest reservation in the northeastern corner of the state. Seven years later, President Theodore Roosevelt, himself a converted conservationist, created Superior National Forest from the lands of this state reserve. That same year, the government of Ontario created the Quetico Provincial Forest Reserve on Canadian forest lands adjacent to Superior National Forest. This simultaneous action of both governments marked the beginning of joint cooperation between the two countries in the protection and management of these companion wildernesses.

Uncontrolled timber cutting was not the only threat to the Quetico-Superior canoe country. With the proliferation of automobiles in the 1920's, Americans were becoming a mobile citizenry, and, as a result, they were demanding a wider range of leisure activities. Businessmen in the rustic hamlets bordering the lakes were quick to grasp the recreational potential of their backyard paradise. All that was needed to make this potential real was an easy means of access – in short, roads to the interior. Joined by the Forest Service, northeastern Minnesota commercial interests lobbied the federal government for funds to construct these essential arteries. While businessmen envisioned the bright glitter of gold at the end of these gasoline rainbows, the foresters saw in the plan a way to insure more effective fire control. It was the kind of short-sighted, political union which has been often repeated in the formulation of United States' natural resource use policy.

Fortunately, not everyone was convinced that resource extraction was the best possible use for the canoe country wilderness. Although land conservation was still a fledgling idea in the nineteen twenties, organizations espousing its virtues were becoming an emerging political force. Founded in 1922, the Izaak Walton League was one such organization. When the road construction plan surfaced, the League promptly engaged the controversy on the side of caution and restraint, vigorously questioning the wisdom for this use of the canoe country. (It was the beginning of the League's unwavering defense of the Quetico-Superior wilderness which has continued to this day.)

Ultimately, the fate of the wilderness was decided in Washington, D.C.– an often repeated occurrence during the 20th Century. In 1926, after four years of hearings, studies and deliberation, Secretary of Agriculture William M. Jardine banned all road construction inside a 640,000 acre lake-studded portion of Superior National Forest. Jardine's proclamation delighted conservationists. The ambitious plan to transform the canoe country wilderness into an easily accessible angler's paradise had been thwarted, at least for the moment.

Recreation was not the Quetico-Superior's only commercial appeal. For some, both forest and water denoted potential profit. The Quetico-Superiors abundant timber was well-suited for wood pulp production to meet the increasing demand for paper. Furthermore, its lakes, if harnessed by a network of damns, could generate a profitable supply of hydroelectricity. These twin possibilities piqued the interest of Minnesota millionaire Edward W. Backus. With his plan devised, Backus arrogantly stomped through the political machinery in both the United States and Canada, working relentlessly to create an industrial empire for himself in the Quetico-Superior region. From 1904 until his death thirty years later, Backus bought and leased timberland and acquired existing dams and undeveloped power sites within the Rainey Lake watershed, using his political clout to cajole and coerce all who stood in his way. Two things were crucial for success: permission from the two governments to raise the water level of the boundary lakes and the acquisition of flowage easements for land flooded by the dams. These were his prize; they would also be his Achilles' heel.

Backus's scheme alarmed a small group of young conservationists. Initially working underground for fear of economic reprisal, they pressed hard for Backus' defeat. Led by a young Minnesota landscape architect, Ernest C. Oberholtzer, the quickly-formed group launched a campaign to bring public attention to the ruinous consequences of their foe's grand design. They had a different vision for the canoe country. It was a wilderness vision, and one which would preserve the lakes and forests in their natural state for the benefit and use of generations to come.

In 1928, Oberholtzer's group formed the Quetico-Superior Council. The Council acted quickly to stop Backus and end forever the notion that the Quetico-Superior region was open for commercial development to the highest bidder.

Immediately, the Council went to Washington, D.C. armed with a legislative initiative that would confront Backus' plan head on. The legislative struggle in Congress was exhausting and at times seemed doomed to failure. For two years legislation supported by the Council floundered in committee. But finally, in 1930, Congress moved on the bill. And later that same year it passed, and President Hoover signed into law the *Shipstead-Nolan Act*. The new law contained two crucial provisions championed by the Council. First, "further alteration of the natural water level" by artificial means within the boarder area watersheds was prohibited. Second, timber within 400 feet of the shoreline could no longer be cut. For Backus, the new law was a major defeat, marking an end to his rapacious scheme, once and for all.

The *Shipstead-Nolan Act* had even broader significance to the emerging wilderness fights nationwide. In his history of this early struggle to save the Quetico-Superior canoe country from development and resource exploitation, R. Newell Searle wrote, "[The Shipstead-Nolan Act] was a measure of national significance...[for] it was the first statute in which Congress explicitly ordered federal land to be retained in its wilderness state."

A country gripped by economic depression is not easily swayed by lofty appeals for forward looking wilderness proposals. Yet, during the 1930's, the Council's Quetico-Superior program moved ahead with steady consistency. The depression years became a period of reaffirmation and consolidation. Minnesota applied the Shipstead-Nolan protections to its forestland in the border area watershed. Furthermore, new lands were added to both the state and federal forest systems, and, for the first time in a bilateral forum, Canada and the United States voiced a need to consider commercial development of the Quetico-Superior region in light of a desire to protect "this last great wilderness." In 1939, The U. S. Forest Service reorganized Superior Roadless Primitive Area into three distinctly separate roadless areas while retaining the basic restrictions in Jardine's original proclamation.

In keeping with the conservationist trend, the Forest Service in 1941 prohibited all timber harvesting in the heart of the canoe country. Although the 360,000 acre no-cut zone removed the most prized portion of the canoe country from the reach of the lumberman's saw, the threat from those who would make this wilderness a resort haven for avid anglers was alive and well. Sizeable tracts of land on interior lakes were still privately owned. As in the 1920's, easy access remained the missing link between dream and reality. The floatplane provided this link.

Resort development in the interior and the aeronautical noise that would make this possible were antithetical to the solitude sought by the wilderness advocates. Much to their dismay, however, nothing prohibited the resort plan or the flights. Even the Forest Service found itself unable to take action; Congress had given it no authority to purchase private land holdings for the sole purpose of fostering a wilderness atmosphere. Although the Isaak Walton League launched an effort to raise funds to purchase these holds, it managed to acquire only a small parcel of the 137,000 acres of the privately owned wilderness land.

The lull was over. The changing times dictated another push for a bold initiative. To repel the threat to the canoe country, two things were essential. First, the Forest Service had to be given the authority and funds to purchase the private land holdings within the wilderness. Second, and more problematic, a legal way to block all flights into the area had to be found.

For two years, Minnesota conservationists lobbied Congress for legislation to broaden the Forest Service's land acquisition authority. (As it stood then, the Forest Service could purchase private land holdings only if the acquisitions directly promoted watershed protection or timber production.) The effort met with stiff local opposition. In this proposed law, northeastern Minnesota businessmen saw the elimination of vacationers and the dollars that they would spend in the communities surrounding the lakes. County governments, on the other hand, feared a contraction of their property-tax base since federal land would be exempt from local taxes.

Despite the local opposition, conservationists secured Congressional approval for their bill in 1948. The *Thye-Blatnik Act* authorized the secretary of agriculture to purchase lands when "their potential or actual development would impair or threaten to impair the unique quality and natural features of the remaining wilderness canoe country." The law also gave the Forest Service a land condemnation authority to be used to force recalcitrant landowners to surrender their holdings. The condemnation authority, which was vigorously used when needed, left behind resentment and fear in the local communities surrounding the wilderness which would resurface with fury thirty years later.

The following year, the fate of the resort development plan was permanently sealed. In December, 1949, President Harry S. Truman, acting on authority granted to him by the

1926 Air Commerce Act, established a 4,000 foot airspace reservation below which aircraft were prohibited from flying except in the rare case of emergency. (The state of Minnesota had acted six months earlier on the issue, banning air landings on all wilderness lakes.) Prospective resort owners litigated the President's executive order, but the federal judge hearing the case sided with the Chief Executive. With the fly-in ban rendering the resort plan untenable, the Forest Service methodically proceeded to acquire the privately held wilderness properties.

In 1958, Superior, Caribou and Little Indian Sioux roadless areas – the triple progeny of the 1938 reorganization – were collectively designated as the Boundary Waters Canoe Area. Six years later, the United States Congress legally validated the concept of wilderness with the passage of the *National Wilderness System Preservation Act of 1964*. The new law, which first appeared as a legislative proposal eight years earlier, placed 9.1 million acres of land in this fledgling wilderness system. Wilderness stalwarts had finally achieved their most sought after goal, and they were elated. The defenders of the canoe country, however, were less jubilant. Although specifically mentioned in the law, the BWCA was not accorded full charter membership in this exclusive wilderness club. This critical exception was to be the source for a vitriolic debate over the proper use of the canoe country, which would result in a new political battle in Minnesota's continuing wilderness war.

A Short Celebration

The Wilderness Act had left little doubt as to Congress's intent. The law clearly stated that the land in the Wilderness System was to "be administrated for the use and enjoyment of the American's people in such manner as will leave them unimpaired for future use and enjoyment as wilderness." Furthermore, administrative policies were to consist of practices which would ensure the preservation of an area's "wilderness character." In the act, wilderness itself is defined poetically as "an area where the earth and its community of life are untrammeled by man, where man himself is a visitor who does not remain."

While Congress's intent is certainly laudable, all was not settled. The seeds for controversy, particularly for the BWCA, were embedded in the new law's more technical language, and this bedeviling fact did not occur by accident.

In 1964, Minnesota Senator Hubert Humphrey was a powerful figure in the United States Senate. Humphrey had long supported the creation of a wilderness system, but only if certain exceptions were made for the BWCA. When the wilderness bill first surfaced in the Eighty-eighth Congress, Humphrey keenly recognized the special problems it posed for his constituents in northeastern Minnesota. While the canoe country's pristine lakes offered a solitary refuge for the wilderness enthusiast, portions of the BWCA also provided a livelihood and recreational playground for the local residents. Most of the people in the small communities bordering the wilderness were anything but wilderness purists. To them, the dense forests and myriad lakes of the BWCA existed to be used, not recklessly, but with an eye fixed on their economic potential. While the haunting call of the loon and the stealthy glide of the canoe might provide the urban wearied soul with solace and rejuvenation, the northern residents of Minnesota knew, all too well, it was the whir of the chain saw and the churn of the outboard motor that provided for their bodily and spiritual sustenance.

For years, logging had existed within designated portions of the BWCA, leading to the distinction between cut and no-cut zones within the canoe country. Furthermore, the lakes, with their national reputation for sporting one of the hardiest populations of game fish in the country, had spawned a sizeable resort business around the edge of the wilderness. Since many anglers came only to fish, the motorboat became essential to this recreational enterprise. Motorized access to the BWCA was important to the local residents, too. Work in the summer was abundant; free time was sparse. A quick and convenient way to arrive at a favorite fishing spot often made the difference between partaking in nature's bounty, or not. In fact, this practice of multiple-use of the canoe country's resources had become an integral part of a way of life greatly cherished by the proud and independent people living in these North Country towns.

If politics is indeed the art of the possible, Hubert Horatio Humphrey was one of its most able practitioners. A master of the twin skills of appeasement and compromise, the Minnesota senator deftly etched his mark on the wilderness law. Wilderness was to remain "untrammeled by man," but its legislative sire was accorded a less propitious fate.

Humphrey offered an amendment to the wilderness bill providing special treatment for the BWCA. In fact, the BWCA is the only area specifically addressed in the Wilderness Act. Although Humphrey's amendment called for the maintenance of the canoe country's "primitive character," it permitted logging and motor boating to continue within its borders.

The Minnesotan had accomplished his goal; the diverse interests were for the moment placated. But this balance was tenuous. How could an ambience of primitiveness exist side-by-side timber cutting and mechanized recreational use? This question was to trouble the canoe country wilderness for the next fifteen years.

As the wilderness bill had worked its way through Congress, Secretary of Agriculture Orville L. Freeman, himself a former Minnesota governor, launched a project to reassess the BWCA's management policies in light of the pending legislation. Freeman appointed a review committee headed by George A. Selke, a former college president and Minnesota state conservation commissioner. The committee promptly focused its attention on the compatibility of logging and wilderness recreation. By late 1964, the report was ready.

The committee's recommendations echoed the new law's sentiments exactly. The BWCA's value as a setting for primitive recreation, the committee concluded, must temper the tone and substance of all management practices. Timber harvesting, however, was an essential management tool needed to achieve this end. "Timber harvesting as a crop is necessary in the BWCA outside the no-cut zone," wrote the committee in a letter to Freeman. "The long-range protection of the Area for recreational purposes requires that the large stands of over-aged timber...should be promptly harvested in a manner which will return the forest to a balanced timber age classification and provide the best example of multiple use forest management." The Selke Committee's words were those of a traditional forest management approach, a notion which would be hotly contested ten years later.

Early in 1964, Freeman had enlarged the no-cut Interior Zone to 512,000 acres, making it nearly one-half of the BWCA's total land area when the Wilderness Act was passed. Based on the Selke Committee's recommendation, the Secretary also earmarked another 100,000 acres for future no-cut consideration. On January 12, 1965, Freeman clearly stated the management direction which would be taken for devising regulations for the BWCA:

> In accepting this recommendation of the Committee, I want to emphasize that the main characteristic of the Canoe Area which is important in wilderness considerations is the spectacular abundance of lakes and streams in a natural setting. The opportunity to use these lakes and streams for primitive-type recreation sets this Area apart from others in the National Forest. Objectives of management must particularly

emphasize the preservation and maintenance of
the primitive character of the Area in the vicinity
of lakes and streams.

In Minnesota, the Izaak Walton League had been leery
of Congress's apparent capitulation to commercial interests
evident in the Wilderness Act. In addition to the Humphrey
amendment, the legislation allowed mineral prospecting and
claim filings to take place on the lands within the Wilderness
System through 1983. The League had considered opposing the Humphrey amendment, but this course was soon
dropped. Its political clout, though rather substantial in
Minnesota, was no match for the state's senior senator on
a national stage. Besides, more was at stake than just their
beloved canoe country. An entire wilderness system which
would protect lands less sheltered than theirs rode tenuously
on the wax and wane of political whim and expediency.
To have vigorously opposed the unpalatable amendment
might have cast the entire legislation into jeopardy. This
was unacceptable. With considerable hesitancy, the League
supported the Wilderness Act in its entirety, while adopting
a wait-and-see attitude toward the worrisome sections in the
legislation. The wait was short.

In the spring of 1969, two businessmen, George W.
St. Clair and Thomas Yawkey, announced their intention
to assess the value of mineral claims which they purport-
edly held in the BWCA. These holdings encompassed about
150,000 acres, fifteen percent of the BWCA land and lakes
included in the Wilderness Act. With tacit approval of the

Forest Service, crews of St. Clair's and Yawkey's geologists entered the BWCA during the early summer. Establishing a base camp in the interior, the geologists conducted surface mineral assays well into the fall.

Shortly after the geologists had commenced their work, the Isaak Walton League began a project of its own. The League moved to persuade Craig Rupp, the Superior National Forest supervisor, to block future activities in the BWCA by the two New Yorkers. Its effort, however, produced only token gestures of concern. The Forest Service notified St. Clair that his equipment would be impounded if it was not immediately removed from the wilderness, and then proceeded to procrastinate over enforcing its September order.

St. Clair's geologists reported that low grade copper and nickel ore existed on his claims, prompting the New York businessman to announce that core drilling samples would be taken the following summer. The operation, he asserted, was essential to determine the potential value of his claims; it also required the use of heavy drilling equipment. This sort of mechanized intrusion into the canoe country – to say nothing of the possible implications of what it might find – was more than Minnesota conservationists could tolerate. In late December 1969, the League filed a request for an injunction against St. Clair in the U. S. District Court in Duluth. Not coincidentally, some thought, the Forest Service impounded St. Clair's equipment several days late.

St. Clair's machinations signaled a greater problem in the Wilderness Act. The law not only appeared to permit the type of activity in which St. Clair was engaged; more disturbingly, it actually mandated that a survey be made of lands within the wilderness system "to determine the mineral value...that may be present."

In January, 1970, a heated statewide debate began over this legislatively mandated survey. Views on the issue spanned the gamut. Predictably, the Northern Environmental Council (an *ad hoc* union of eighteen conservationist groups from Minnesota, Wisconsin, and northern Michigan) adamantly opposed both the mineral survey and any subsequent mining which might result from it in and around the BWCA. At the other extreme, University of Minnesota professor Dr. George Weaton, testifying before the state senate's Public Domains Committee hearing on the issue, went so far as to advocate mining within the wilderness if marketable quantities of minerals were discovered. Weaton's tersely dismissive remarks such as "minerals are where you find them" and "mining and conservation are not incompatible," enraged many in the state's conservationist community.

A war of words also commenced between state officials and elected representatives. Responding to a conservation department attorney's assertion that Minnesota would never support a policy permitting mineral exploration on the 100,000 acres of private holdings scattered throughout the BWCA, Duluth State Senator Raymond Higgins asserted that mineral holdings within the canoe country "could be worth millions of dollars to the state," and to impede the survey would be tantamount to public confiscation of these legally owned claims. (Interestingly, it was later revealed that Higgins himself owned part interest in mineral rights on 117 acres in the BWCA. This revelation forced Higgin's resignation from the Public Domains Committee, and he later ceded his mineral holdings to the federal government.)

The issue came to a head in May when the United States Geological Survey and the United States Bureau of Mines, the two agencies assigned to conduct the survey mandated in the Wilderness Act, announced a plan to begin their own core drilling operations in the BWCA. In making the announcement, the agencies pointed to the law's requirement that a report based on the completed survey be submitted to Congress by 1977. The May announcement mobilized opposition to all forms of mining activities in the wilderness.

In the spring of the year, conservationists, state officials, and members of Minnesota's congressional delegation pressured Secretary of the Interior Walter Hickel to cancel the drilling plan outright. Their efforts resulted in a partial victory. In June 1970, the federal government temporarily postponed the plan to drill in the BWCA. Still, the implication of mineral holdings on wilderness lands had been made graphically evident. The need for an outright ban of all forms of mineral prospecting in the BWCA was abundantly clear.

With the mining case awaiting trial, the State of Minnesota joined with the League in the litigation against St. Clair and the federal government. Minnesota's motives were two-fold. The federal government had challenged the League's legal standing in the case, a fundamental point of law which requires that a party to a lawsuit have a clear and demonstrable interest in the outcome of the case. In entering the suit on the League's side, the state intended to negate any consequence from an adverse ruling on the League's legal standing. As it was, federal district court Judge Phillip Neville rejected the federal government's challenge, declaring, "[The League] is not a 'Johnny-come-lately' or an *ad hoc* organization and its interest in the wilderness movement is continuing basic and deep."

But Minnesota had an even more compelling reason for joining this legal fight. The state still owned large pockets of land in northeastern Minnesota. It also retained jurisdiction over the water in the BWCA, and access to the area over its lakes and streams was the only viable method of travel in this wilderness since road building had been banned by Jardine in 1926. Regardless of what the federal government did, Minnesota controlled the requisite key to mining ingress and egress in the BWCA.

State officials feared that if a monetary value for these privately held claims could be established through core drilling assays, both the state and the federal government might be faced with two equally distasteful alternatives: the purchase of the mineral rights from the people who held claims or the permitting of those rights to be exercised – in short, mining in the wilderness. For the state, the purchase of private mineral holdings posed potentially dire fiscal consequences. Phi Olfelt, the state's attorney litigating the case, later revealed that state officials felt St. Clair's motive from the start had been to establish a basis for demanding compensation for his holdings. Why else, Olfeld reasoned, would St. Clair undertake such an expensive operation in an area for which permission to mine would never be granted?

Wishing to avoid this dilemma, at least in the short run, the state took the initiative in the case. If the legitimacy of St. Clair's holdings could be successfully contested, the immediate threat would be eliminated.

In early 1972, Olfeld delivered the state's argument before Judge Neville. It was no secret that during the late nineteenth and early twentieth centuries a practice of fraudulent filings for federal land ran rampant throughout northern Minnesota. No fewer than three federal laws allowed individuals to obtain homesteading land grants on federal land. These laws required that the grant's recipient actively use the land. Frequently, however, the homesteads remained undeveloped, and the mineral rights were routinely sold to large mining concerns before the ownership of the land reverted back to the federal government. At the turn of the century, state officials had apprised Washington of this prolific scam; however, federal officials took only rare action. Presenting to the court extensive documentation from archival records, the state proved, irrefutably, that most of St. Clair's holdings had been originally obtained illegally. As the state saw it, since the original claims were fraudulently obtained, St. Clair's holdings belonged not to him, but to the public, thus making drilling a moot issue.

Judge Neville complimented the state on its thorough research. A preponderance of evidence did, indeed, support the state's claim of fraud. Unfortunately, one hitch existed. The six-year statute of limitations for fraud had long expired. No matter how the defendant's holdings were first acquired, he was now home free, at least so far as his right to retain them was concerned. Besides, wrote Neville, even if the state's argument had merit, it was the federal government upon whom fraud had been perpetrated, and, hence, it was the federal government who must bring the action. With the state's assertion rebuffed, Neville set the trial date for September 15, 1972.

Things Get Complicated

When it rains, it pours, the old saw laments. Those who have traveled the canoe country can attest to the verity of this gnome; and those who were active in the wilderness's political tumult in the early seventies may well have voiced a similar repine. With the mining issue in court, two other problems raised their troublesome heads: logging and snowmobiling. Coupled with the mining controversy, they served to confirm the initial concern over the Wilderness Act's vexing contradictions.

In the spring of 1971, a forest fire swept over portions of the BWCA along an old logging road called the Echo Trail. Crossing one major canoe route, the fire lasted four days and burned 16,000 acres of primarily coniferous forest. It was later determined that the fire had started from live coals left from a Forest Service slash-burn operation on cutover land. Press reports on the Little Indian Sioux fire, as it was called, stimulated the public's curiosity.

During the summer, the Echo Trail was busier than usual. Some visitors drove down the sinuous gravel road simply to see the fire's charred remains, while others enjoyed the challenge and solitude of a canoe trip on a little used route that began on the Little Indian Sioux and Nina-Moose Rivers and had been publicized as a result of the fire. To the surprise of many, they also discovered logging in the wilderness. The existence of timber harvesting in portions of the BWCA had not been concealed by the Forest Service, however, until the spring fire it had attracted little public attention.

The Minnesota Public Interest Research Group (MPIRG), a political action, student organization, took particular interest in this commercial venture. During the summer, MPIRG representatives made inquiries into the extent of the logging activity being conducted in the BWCA. They were alarmed by their findings. Not only were several large tracks – totaling 10,000 acres – currently under contract to be cut, but much of the acreage contained stately stands of virgin forest on land never before logged.

One area partially burned by the Little Indian Sioux fire was a 160 acre stand of hundred-year-old red pine located next to a portage leading to a major canoe route. Disturbingly, MPIRG discovered that U. S. Steel Corporation owned the land that trees were on, and that the company had scheduled the timber to be cut. The student group promptly moved to stop the harvest.

Now, the preservation of this small track of forest may have appeared inconsequential to most, but its survival had considerable significance for ecologists who studied forest succession. Since the regenerative process of a red pine forest was not fully understood, the scientists wanted to preserve the site as a natural laboratory where studies could be conducted. In so doing, they hoped to find an answer to a perplexing question: how did red pine samplings – a shade intolerant species requiring considerable light to grow – mature when a forest's overstory shrouded them from the sun's rays. One hypothesis stated that periodic forest fires both thinned the overstory and fertilized the soil thus allowing new growth to occur. Consequentially, the stand of burnt trees had transformed this site into a good place to study the process first hand.

The strategy to save the trees seemed simple: purchase the land from this giant steel company. MPIRG, itself not in the land buying business, contacted The Nature Conservancy. At the time, The Nature Conservancy was a low profile conservationist organization whose primary mission was the purchase and stewardship of parcels of land which possessed unique natural characteristics. The Conservancy was interested and contacted U. S. Steel. A correspondence ensued, but the negotiations for the land's purchase soon fell into a state of confusion and delay. Although one Minneapolis newspaper reported that an agreement had been reached and then promptly cancelled by the steel company, as it was, the effort had never gotten beyond the letter writing stage. Edward Bray, the Conservancy representative handling the matter, later recalled, "It was only after lengthy efforts that I was able to get any response from [the company]." When the response finally came it was, to say the least, disappointing. U. S. Steel informed the Conservancy that the trees had already been salvaged. The Conservancy followed with an offer to purchase the land anyway. This offer, too, was ignored. The steel company never explained its reasons for refusing to sell the property.

The imminent threat to the last remaining stands of virgin forest and the insensitivity of the corporate giant to the needs of science propelled MPIRG forward. Early in 1972, the student environmentalists asked the Forest Service to suspend BWCA contracts on the land which supported virgin forest. Superior National Forest officials in Duluth, however, denied the request. MPIRG appealed, first to the forest chief and then to the secretary of agriculture. Expectedly, Secretary of Agriculture Earl Butz supported his subordinates' decision, stating firmly, "Revocation of existing contracts would work an economic hardship on the people whose livelihood is dependent on harvesting or processing the timber from the sale."

MPIRG's trundle through the bureaucratic maze had been both frustrating and disappointing. Still, the young Minnesotans were not yet ready to quit the fight. One path, litigation, had remained unexplored. That summer, MPIRG began preparation for the lawsuit that they hoped would permanently banish the disquieting sound of the chainsaw from the canoe country wilderness.

In the winter of 1972, a third issue literally slid into what was becoming a rather heated debate over the canoe country wilderness. In February, President Richard Nixon issued Executive Order 11644, banning snowmobiles on lands within the Wilderness System. Unlike motorboats, snowmobiles were not mentioned in the BWCA section of the Wilderness Act. Nevertheless, Secretary Butz had sanctioned snowmobile use in the BWCA, probably reasoning that motors in the winter are no more offensive than those in the summer, and motors in the summer the law clearly allowed. Nixon's order apparently reversed his secretary's ruling.

Despite the clarity of the presidential order, the fortunes of motorized frolics across snow-covered lakes remained uncertain. The residents of northeastern Minnesota were livid over the ban. It was one thing to contract the basis for their livelihood, but it was altogether something else to end a popular pastime in this land of harsh and long winters. The snowmobile ban took on a symbolic meaning of its own. The issue came uncomfortably close to something held religiously sacred by the northern Minnesotans, a way of life unencumbered by the generally accepted imperatives and constraints of twentieth century society.

The protest from the north was vocal. And the executive order was suspended, pending further consideration. At this point, a climate of indecision gripped efforts to resolve the controversy. Over the next three years the federal bureaucracy vacillated, imposing and rescinding the ban, repeatedly.

O Canada

While wilderness advocates in the United States worked to repel each emerging threat to the BWCA, Canadians were quietly taking up their own cause. At the turn of the century, logging was the main commercial enterprise in the Quetico. Shetland-Clark Lumber Ltd. and later Jim Mathieu Lumber Ltd. dominated timber harvesting in the Quetico until the mid 1960's, when, as a result of the introduction of modern logging techniques by multinational timber companies, Mathieu was forced out of business. Before departing, however, Mathieu Lumber registered a sizeable impact on the area. Between 1918 and 1946 alone, the period of Mathieu's dominance in the area, the Ministry of Natural Resources in Ontario estimates that 520 million board feet of red and white pine was cut in the park.

In 1943, a 900 square mile recreational preserve was created in the Quetico, known as Hunters Island. Yet, half of what today comprises the Canadian canoe country still remained opened to logging. In 1963, Ontario-Minnesota Pulp and Paper Company Ltd., a subsidiary of America's giant Boise Cascade, acquired cutting rights to 420 square miles of park land. The same year, Mathieu Lumber followed suit, acquiring the right to cut timber on 468 square miles in the Quetico. In 1967, when Mathieu folded, its cutting rights were purchased by the Boise Cascade subsidiary. By 1970, the American controlled company held the timber rights to half of Canada's canoe country wilderness.

Ontario's policy of permitting wholesale timber harvesting in the Quetico alarmed the Algonquin Wildlands League, a Toronto based conservationist group. Initially formed to combat logging in Algonquin Park, a protected canoe area in eastern Ontario, the League spearheaded a campaign to stop timber operations in the Quetico. Unlike in Minnesota, its efforts achieved a quick response from the Ontario government.

In June 1970, the Department of Land and Forests, the agency responsible for letting and supervising logging contracts, formed an advisory committee to examine its park management policies. The twelve member Quetico Provincial Park Advisory Committee held a series of hearings in Fort Francis, Atikokan and Thunder Bay, the three northwestern Ontario communities most directly affected by logging, and also in the provinces largest city, Toronto. The hearings attracted considerable attention. At one preceding, the Committee took testimony from 144 witnesses and received 263 written briefs and some 4,500 letters, most favoring full wilderness status for the Quetico.

The majority of the testimony focused on the logging issue. On this issue, conservationists and timber industry representatives differed greatly. As the timber industry saw it, the forest was a renewable resource whose careful management perpetuated both its commercial value and recreational appeal. In fact, the industry representatives repeatedly maintained that the periodic cutting of "overly mature timber" enhanced rather than degraded the quality of the wilderness experience enjoyed by the many canoeists who travelled in the park. One witness, Bruce Seppala, strongly challenged the notion that a resource of that size should be set aside solely for wilderness recreation. Representing the company which held sizable Quetico timber contracts, Seppala asserted that the forest should be thought of "in terms of [its] use-benefit ratio" and that one of those benefits was the economics derived from responsibly managed logging in the area. To make his point stick, the logging representative painted a picture of the dire consequences which would certainly befall the Quetico if logging were eliminated. Unequivocally, Seppela warned the Committee that "vast stands of timber would be subject to the ravage of insects, disease and fire... Instead of a park," he contended, "the area becomes a disaster of jack strawed dead sticks and it is downright criminal to let this sort of thing happen."

Conservationists saw things differently. Sigurd Olson, a northeastern Minnesotan who had written extensively on the Quetico-Superior canoe country, most eloquently presented their position. Olson had been a faithful warrior in the Quetico-Superior struggle and possessed a deep understanding of the ecology of the region. Then in his seventies, he did not share Seppala's vision of a wilderness that would self-destruct in the absence of man's taming influence. "This area, as ecologists look at it, is what is known as fire ecology," Olson explained. "This country is as it is because of fire....I look at this matter of therapeutic logging with a rather jaundice eye," he said, maintaining that such a practice would drastically transform the wilderness's "fragile and inter-related ecology." Olson concluded his testimony on a philosophical note, one that struck a rare chord of truth for many of those sitting in the hearing room. "This is an era of environmental awareness," he reminded the Committee, "where it becomes very important to preserve the last relics of wilderness...not for ourselves, but for generations to come. The Quetico is really a museum, just as much a museum as though it was within a glass case in Ottawa and Toronto."

The numerous witnesses at the hearings differed in approach and meaning, yet most acknowledged the value of wilderness recreation. Nevertheless, least we forget that there are a few amongst us who still look at a tree only to see board feet, or covet a wilderness landscape solely for what lies beneath it in the ground, the remarks of one witness, Robert Campbell of the Prospectors' and Developers' Association, are worth repeating here in their entirety:

> **Mr. Campbell:** *All mining can be controlled by good house-keeping...This province just cannot afford to leave a mineral deposit unmined any more than the land between Winnipeg and the foothills could have been left unfarmed. In my estimation, anyone wanting to enjoy the mystique of the wilderness would do better to go elsewhere, other than to the so-called park.*

> **Committee Member John E. Stokes:** *Mr. Campbell, in your opinion should any of the land in Quetico be set aside as wilderness?*

> **Mr. Campbell:** *I really don't think a very big area should be set aside for that reason...There are a lot of places people can go, say northern Ontario, which I don't think will ever be lived on or settled on and will only be used for lumbering, trapping and so on.*

Mr. Stokes: *Could it follow that you are opposed to the concept of national parks where any resource exploration is prohibited?*

Mr. Campbell: *Yes, I am.*

Mr. Stokes: *You are opposed to national parks?*

Mr. Campbell: *Yes.*

Vice-Chairman Clifford McIntosh: *Mr. Campbell, you said 2% of the people [who camp in parks] go into the forest. Is that right?*

Mr. Campbell: *Yes.*

Mr. McIntosh: *What's the source of this information?*

Mr. Campbell: *The source of this information is really hearsay. What I mean is if you added up all the numbers of people who use the camp sites that people arrive at by car, and the people who actually go on canoe trips or walk more than a quarter of a mile away from a river, that they would be a pretty small number.*

Mr. McIntosh: *I could say 52% with as much validity in terms of hard fact. 52%, I could say the same kind of thing...[your] 2%, what's the validity of that?*

Mr. Campbell: Oh, well I think the source of it came out by one of the speakers at the Algonquin Park hearings...It was probably one of the lumber

people. I don't think it would be a conservationist...
But I would say it's right.

Later in his testimony, while crediting mining with
opening the North American West, the mining representative offered still another enlightened view to the Committee.
"Now, if you leave the country absolutely empty [where]
there is no development at all," reasoned Campbell, "It is of
very little use to anyone and I don't think this country with
so many people on welfare can afford that sort of standard."

In May, 1972, only one month after the hearings concluded, the provincial government ended all logging in
Quetico Provential Park. One year later, the Committee
released its final report. The report was unusually straight-
forward, and its findings and recommendations delighted
conservationists in both Canada and the United States. "The
Government," wrote the Committee, "[should] adopt and
affirm as a policy for Quetico Park its preservation in perpetuity for the people of Ontario as a wilderness area not
adversely affected by human activities." This policy, advised
the committee, should emanate from a new park's land category which would confer upon the Quetico full wilderness status.

The Advisory committee's report was important for two
reasons. First, this was the first time in Ontario that an official
government body unequivocally acknowledged the value of
wilderness preservation. And second, the Committee's recommendations encouraged conservationists in the States,
then immersed in a morass of seemingly irresolvable issues,
to press on toward their ambitious goal.

In both countries the push would continue, although in a starkly different manner. Ontario, with at times almost slumberous certitude, would methodically plod on arriving at last at a point reached by its southern neighbor. But it was in the United States that the wilderness struggle would weave a labyrinthine drama of intrigue.

Back in the States

With the Advisory Committee's report now a matter of record and the BWCA logging and snowmobile dispute in abeyance, the St. Clair case went back to court. The September, 1972, proceedings lasted only one day, but Judge Neville was left with a plethora of arguments to sort and consider.

In tandem, the Izaak Walton League and the state of Minnesota submitted that the historical thrust of both state and federal policy led to one irrefutable conclusion: the BWCA had been intentionally zoned to prohibit all activities which threatened the integrity of its unique wilderness character. Unquestionably, mining was an intrusive activity precluded by the precedent of past policy. Although St. Clair and others would be denied access to the potential profits from their legal holdings, this, claimed the League and the State, could not be offered as reason for the court to rule in their favor. Zoning was a firmly established police power of government, and the federal courts had ruled in a number of cases that the authority was properly exercised even when some property values were adversely affected.

St. Clair's attorneys countered by pointing out to the judge that the Wilderness Act specifically permitted mineral prospecting on the system's lands. In fact, it was clearly Congress's intent to allow the continuation of some form of mining inside the wilderness; the law's own words were proof of this. Yet, even if Congress had prohibited all wilderness mining, by blocking access to St. Clair's legal holdings the government would be denying the defendant his constitutional due process property rights.

The fourth participant in the trial was the federal government, who still sided with St. Clair, but for a different reason. The federal government's position rested on a prosaic point of administrative procedure. The government's attorney pointed out to the court that St. Clair had submitted a request to the Forest Service for permission to take core drilling samples on BWCA lands. The agency had yet to act on the application. Until the St. Clair's request was acted on, the government argued, all other questions in this case were being litigated prematurely.

By January, Neville was ready with his decision. Proceeding with the steadiness of a man on a mission, the judge observed, "There can be no question that full mineral development and mining will destroy and negate the wilderness or most of it." Even if perfect land reclamation were possible, the regenerative process would likely span generations. For this reason alone, Neville concluded, the impact of mining in the wilderness would be irreversible. Wilderness and mining were therefore "opposing values and anathema each to the other," asserted the judge.

But how would Neville reconcile his understanding of wilderness's prerogatives with the provision for mineral prospecting, clearly stated in the Wilderness Act? The judge disposed of this problem with surprisingly little difficulty. If the act were to be considered something other than a mere "exercise in futility," reasoned Neville, it must follow that Congress intended to make wilderness paramount. "A mineral resource developer cannot proceed without making use of the surface of the land. Any use of the surface for exploration of minerals becomes an unreasonable use because the surface is no longer wilderness and is irreversibly and irretrievably destroyed for generations to come." Even prospecting runs contrary to the law's intent, ruled the judge, since it "follow(s) as an *a fortiori,* that removal of ore is the next step."

As for the federal government's procedural argument, Neville's substantive ruling prohibiting mining on wilderness lands rendered the outcome of this bureaucratic formality meaningless. Regardless of the documentation submitted by St. Clair to support his claim, the Forest Service could reach but one conclusion: no prospecting in the BWCA whatsoever.

Neville's neatly packaged decision received plaudits from environmentalists nationwide. One group in particular, MPIRG, took close notice of the judicial edict. Frustrated by the federal government's obstinacy on the logging issue, the student group had filed suit in federal court, seeking to enjoin any cutting of virgin forest until the Forest Service had completed its environmental impact statement on the existing contracts. With the Neville decision now a matter of record and their trial ongoing, MPRIG reassessed its position.

The implications of the St. Clair case were apparent to MPIRG's attorney, Chuck Dayton. If mining could be disposed of so tidily, why could the logging of virgin forest not be handled in a similar manner? MPIRG decided to go for broke and amended its original motion, asking the court for a complete ban on the execution of the contested contracts.

The MPIRG case had been assigned to Federal District Judge Miles Lord. Dayton's argument's before the court closely paralleled the Neville decision. The Minneapolis attorney contended that the wilderness law and subsequent administrative actions had clearly provided for the protection of the BWCA's "primitive character," and the virgin forest, a natural feature unaltered by man, fell within this umbrella of protection. *Ipso jure* the disputed contracts must be voided, Dayton asserted.

Several days later, Judge Lord stopped the logging pending the outcome of the Forest Service's environmental impart statement. Although the judge stopped short of voiding the timber contracts entirely, in his written decision he left little doubt about what he expected the impact study to show. Pointedly, Lord wrote, "Since the evidence clearly showed that logging destroyed the primitive character of the area involved and the Wilderness Act mandates that the primitive character of the BWCA be maintained, the court must conclude that there is a strong possibility and, in fact, a probability, that future logging in the BWCA will be entirely prohibited or be restricted to non-virgin forest areas under the Forest Service's new BWCA Management Plan."

Environmentalists were elated. By the spring of 1973, mining had been banned completely, while logging, at least in virgin forest, appeared soon to follow. Even the proscription of snowmobiling within the wilderness, though then in a state of uncertainty, had the weight of a presidential order behind it and thus, seemingly, was on its way out, as well. In their wildest fantasies of right over might, the wilderness defenders could not have expected more.

Things fall apart

In early August, 1973, the environmental community began to sense that their gains were not as secure as they had seemed several months earlier. The pendulum was starting its backwards swing, and the time it would mark was that of a bygone era. In August, the Forest Service released its new BWCA Management Plan: the logging of virgin forest was restricted, but not eliminated. Ten months later, the Eighth Circuit Court of Appeals overturned Neville's decision on BWCA mining. Accepting the federal government's position on primary jurisdiction, the appellate court stated that the Forest Service must first act on St. Clair's drilling permit request before a ruling on the case's merits could be rendered. In the interim, St. Clair had died, and the required documentation supporting the permit request was never supplied.

In the same month as the appellate court ruling, International Nickel Company (INCO), a New York based mining combine, disclosed its plan to develop an open-pit, copper-nickel mine bordering the BWCA. The plan called for the use of 5,000 acres for the mine, a concentrating plant, and an impoundment facility to be used to dispose of its toxic tailings; it also offered an appealing carrot of 800 jobs to this economically depressed region of Minnesota.

Environmentalists and state officials were alarmed over the mine's proposed site next to the South Kawishiwi River, a river that flowed directly into the BWCA. INCO's plan presented a new wrinkle to the mining controversy. Even if Neville's ruling had held, it would not have prevented mining adjacent to the wilderness. But most mining observers knew, all to well, the tainting effect of mining could be felt far beyond the mine's site.

A coalition of environmental groups twenty-six strong was quickly formed to fight the INCO plan. But the issue was more than company profit versus wilderness preservation. Pure and simple, the livelihood of the common working man was at stake as well.

Unemployment in northeastern Minnesota in the early seventies ran well above the national average. (In Ely, a small town on the southern edge of the BWCA, real unemployment was reported to be around 17% when the INCO announcement broke.) Opposition to the mining plan coming largely from the southern part of the state created an atmosphere of suspicion and animosity between these north woods communities and the Twin Cities area. The hostility would last for the duration of the struggle.

The INCO controversy rapidly accelerated resentment in northeastern Minnesota. People in the region viewed the opposition to the mining proposal as an intrusion by outsiders into local economic affairs. Showing evidence of the building tension, Ely's mayor, Doctor Joseph Grahek, responding to a reporter's question, scolded, "Who are these people in Minneapolis and St. Paul who want to tell us what to do? They want a Mecca for themselves up here at our expense."

Although patently parochial, it was a point of view that the people in the north felt deserved some consideration. After all, they endured the harsh winters in order to live in this area. Many of them used the recreational resource that was at the center of this fight and they resented the suggestion that they had no interest in protecting it. But most irritating was the perception of a condescending tone coming from the environmental community as it steadily advanced its preservationist message, while dismissing, out of hand, what local residents felt were valid economic concerns.

Despite their complaints of meddling and vows of pure intentions, the local people never received a sympathetic ear from the media. With environmentalists applying constant pressure and the state threatening more stringent mining legislation, INCO eventually abandoned its mining plan in January, 1976. The costs were too high and the hassles too great, the company explained as it made the announcement. INCO departed, but not without leaving an indelible awareness of the ever present threat that hovered over this fragile wilderness.

A Critical Alliance

With the threads of protection unraveling everywhere, environmentalists regrouped to stave off further losses. Facing another court battle as a result the Forest Service's unacceptable management plan, MPIRG sought to enhance its political clout. Early in 1974 the student group began to lobby the Sierra Club, a national organization that advocated for preservationist causes. If MPIRG could enlist the Sierra Club's active support, it might be enough to tip the scales in their favor.

By August, MPIRG's efforts had paid off. Brock Evans, a Sierra Club Washington lobbyist, flew to Minnesota to attend a strategy meeting held at a summer cabin on Burnside Lake just west of Ely. At the two day meeting, Evans and the Minnesota environmentalists charted a course of action which would carry the flow of events over the next four trying years. The meeting began with the group methodically dissecting its successes and failures. Administrative appeals had definitely been unsuccessful. Although the courts had been receptive, even favorable, to their position, drawbacks existed there, too. The appellate court's ruling in the St. Clair case had placed the likelihood of a judicial solution in limbo. Besides, the courts with their lengthy appeals process promised, at best, a protracted end to the controversy. The group concluded that more was needed. The time seemed right for a major and, hopefully, decisive legislative thrust; and with its new ally having Washington connections, the prospects for success seemed very good indeed.

The clandestine gathering adjourned with a battle plan: administrative appeals would be pressed only as a stopgap measure; litigation on the logging controversy would be vigorously prosecuted; but now more time and money would be directed toward Washington, Congress, and, it was hoped a propitious outcome.

The Lake Burnside meeting reshaped the nature of the BWCA struggle. Until then, environmentalists had been on the defensive, repelling one threat after another. Now, with a strategy devised, they were confident that this pattern would be reversed. "The green mafia," a name given to the group by Chuck Dayton, would launch an all-out offensive to preserve the canoe country exclusively as wilderness. And preservationists they would remain for the duration of the fight. This time, their long –sought after dream of wilderness purity would not be foiled.

In September, 1974, MPIRG returned to court to seek a continuance of the injunction and to establish a date for the forthcoming logging trial. In August, the Forest Service had finalized its new BWCA Master Plan, thus freeing the disputed timber contracts from their judicial binds. Judge Lord was miffed by the Forest Service's failure to heed his earlier admonishment, and from the bench he made his feelings known in no uncertain terms. Borrowing a reference from Dr. Seuss book, the judge quipped, "The court is not unmindful of the warning of Lorax about the Oncelers of the world and their penchant for cutting down the truffula trees to make thneeds," concluding that, "irreparable harm will occur to the plaintiffs if logging activities are conducted in the BWCA pending a trial on that matter." The injunction was extended and a trial date was set for late November.

As Dayton and his staff reviewed volumes of documents to prepare for the trial, Evans and Myron "Bud" Heinselman were fast pursuing a different tack. (It was Heinselman's Burnside Lake cabin where the summer strategy meeting had been held. Heinselman had retired early from the Forest Service to engage in the wilderness fight. In fact, he had been one of Dayton's key expert witnesses at the first logging trial. And now he was about to play a starring role as events unfolded.)

In the closing days of its ninety-third session, Congress was considering a major piece of wilderness legislation, the Eastern Wilderness bill. Why not attach an amendment to the bill that would end BWCA logging entirely? This, however, would not be easy. Hope for success hinged on gaining the support of northeastern Minnesota's congressman, John Blatnik. Blatnik was a deft politician who had maintained his twenty-eight year hold on the eighth-district seat by faithfully representing the interest of his North Country constituents. A no-cut stand by Blatnik would not be well received by the voters. Yet, Blatnik had already announced his retirement from Congress, and this Evans and Heinselman hoped would work in their favor.

Heiselman approached the lame-duck congressman with a proposition: in exchange for sponsoring the amendment banning BWCA logging, Blatnik would be accorded a hero's status in the environmental community. Unfortunately, Blatnik had no interest in such a distinction. The two met several times, but to no avail. The 1975 Eastern Wilderness Act was signed into law with no mention of BWCA logging.

Later, Heinselman accused Blatnik of reneging on a promise to support the amendment. At the time, rumors had circulated in private, and were alluded to in the press, that Blatnik had backed out at the last moment because of pressure from economic interests in northeastern Minnesota. (At the time, Blatnik's former aide and close friend, Thomas Smrekar, was the public affairs director for Potlatch Lumber Company, one of the defendants in the upcoming logging trial.) The outgoing congressman, however, flatly denied that he had ever agreed to support Heinselman's amendment, maintaining that his position on the logging issue had been absolutely consistent with his record on such matters.

All and all, the brief interlude with the legislative process was a disappointment but not a disaster. The prospects for a favorable judicial resolution of the logging issue seemed good. Still, the episode pointed to the difficulties which lay ahead. On the road to Washington the wilderness advocates would encounter many obstacles, not the least of which was Blatnik's successor, James Oberstar, an able adversary in his own right.

In late November, 1974, the logging trial began and would last through the new year. MPIRG, joined by the Sierra Club, took the early initiative. Offering numerous documents to support their position, the preservationist attacked both the adequacy of the Forest Service environmental impact statement and its own BWCA Management Plan. Government witness testimony was thoroughly dissected. At each step in the rule-making process, Dayton and the Sierra Club's attorneys probed the witnesses' every action, every thought and, above all, every motive that went into preparing the contested documents.

But the issue was much larger than paper inclusions and omissions. In his opening remarks to the court, MPIRG attorney Chuck Dayton made this abundantly clear. "Our position," asserted Dayton, "is that the Wilderness Act is intended to save wilderness not only for recreation but for its own sake, and just preserving wilderness for people's use is less than Congress intended." The outcome of the trial would hinge upon this central assertion.

The defendants saw it differently. Speaking for the defense, Boise Cascade's attorney Curtis Roy contended that Congress had no intention of conferring full wilderness status on the BWCA. Why else, Curtis asked, would it have been treated separately in the wilderness law? Pointing to the legislative phrase "particularly in the vicinity of lakes, streams and portages" – a phrase that went hand in hand with the law's charge to maintain the area's primitive character – Roy asserted that the deliberate inclusion of this phrase "reinforced the idea that we are to maintain the BWCA only as a wilderness waterway area." (This distinction was crucial to the case, since 90 percent of the BWCA canoe routes already lay within the no-cut Interior Zone, and, therefore, the cutting of virgin forest would not noticeably affect the "wilderness waterway area.")

Although the court heard testimony from only twelve witnesses, the trial lasted eighteen days and amassed over two thousand pages of transcript. The players in the courtroom drama frequently made their feelings known, often heatedly. Logging company attorneys objected repeatedly to Dayton's characterization of the issues and his lines of questioning. Dayton struck frequently at government witnesses and particularly hard at former Superior National Forest chief, John Anderson; and the judge jousted with just about everyone.

At its heart, the trial was really one of definitions. Time and again, the attorneys and witnesses meandered back and forth over the vague concepts of wilderness, primitive character, and virgin forest. The courtroom players repeatedly let one crucial distinction after another slip from their grasp. At one point, however, a voice of homespun reason emerged from the fray to bring a badly needed perspective to this mass of confusion. Ron Walls, an Ely attorney for Norman Kainz, a local mill owner, rose to his feet and offered a rare, but lucid contribution. "If I understand all of this correctly, your honor," quipped Walls, "wilderness is a place where the hand of man has never set foot." Even Lord, who from time to time during the trial offered his own renditions of comic relief, had to laugh at Walls' jocose definition.

It was of little surprise that the decision fell as it did, squarely with the preservationists. Early in the trial Consolidated Paper's attorney, Joe Walters, had vehemently objected to Dayton's questions, which had probed into the minutest aspects of the Forest Service's decision-making process. When Walter's contended that a determination of the substantive adequacies of the impact statement and master plan was beyond the scope of the trial – adding emphatically that one could "nit-pick all the way down the line" while accomplishing nothing but to bring the wheels of government "to a complete stop" – the Minnesota jurist interrupted to make plain his focus in this matter. "When I am talking about this case and thinking of it, I am thinking of the long pull of our struggle to stay alive on the surface of this earth and preserve mankind itself," snorted Lord from the bench. "And I am not talking about some temporary inconvenience, a detour, or a temporary bridge, or some noise pollution, or somebody might not like to hear trucks driving as they paddle their canoe down a creek. I am thinking of the long haul." Dayton could continue this line of questioning.

By August, 1975, the judge had severed from this mass of materials whatever well concealed kernels of truth that may have existed. His fifty-eight page decision painstakingly summarized the critical features of the disputed contracts and the environmental impact statement and master plan decision-making process.

In his testimony, Heinselman maintained that virgin forest was "any forest primarily the product of natural forces that never [had] been subject to direct alteration by man." In the final analysis, Lord's verdict hinged on his acceptance of the former Forest Service employee's definition of virgin forest and the judge's interpretation of the Wilderness Act. "This Court is convinced," the judge wrote, "that an adequate

EIS would show that logging destroyed the primitive character of the BWCA and that it should not be used as a management tool."

The injunction was made permanent; virgin forest would remain uncut. The environmentalists were back in business, and the business of wilderness was beginning to boom.

Those damn machines

If by now, the Forest Service was feeling somewhat maligned, the snowmobile issue only added further to its woes. On this, the agency found itself caught in the middle of a no-win situation. Butz had ruled snowmobiling permissible in the BWCA, but Nixon's executive order appeared to countermand his secretary's decision. Yet, the BWCA had been treated as a special case in the Wilderness Act. A recreational use prohibited in other wilderness areas, namely motorboating, was permitted in the canoe country.

Considering the act's exception, and with a mixed message from Butz and Nixon, the Forest Service permitted snowmobile use on designated routes until 1980 in its BWCA management plan. When the plan was unveiled, preservationists strongly objected and lodged an immediate appeal. They claimed that snowmobiling in the BWCA was an unacceptable insult to the area's primitive character. As all awaited Lord's mid-May decision, John McGuire, the Forest Service chief, again barred snowmobiles from the BWCA.

Logging and mining may have provided a livelihood for the people of northeastern Minnesota, but it was the recreational amenities of the region which lay closest to their hearts. Tampering with these amenities was, for many, sufficient cause for a call to arms. (Chuck Dayton later claimed that it was the snowmobile rather than the logging issue which really "galvanized the opposition.")

Feelings in the north ran strong on this issue. The snow-mobile ban seemed like sheer nonsense, since few people braved the harsh North Country winter to use the wilderness for little else. For the local people, this whole "primitive character" business was getting way out of hand.

Despite the growing tension between the environmentalist "outsiders" and the local people who lived in the region, the north woods residents had not yet lost their sense of humor over the contentious issues. Attendees at an Ely town meeting passed a proposal for the creation of a "Greater Metropolitan Canoe Area" in the Twin Cities area. Predictably, the proposal banned the use of snowmobiles and motorboats, and prohibited further cutting of timber in the seven country region. Natural forces must be allowed to run their course, they added. Interestingly, the Twin Cities area was beset by an infestation of Dutch Elm diseases and the infected trees were being removed with great regularity. The tongue-in-cheek proposal, which reappeared several times in the state legislature, made a point that the people of northeastern Minnesota felt was long overdue.

But on snowmobiling, Washington was itself the source of the problem, and thus it was also the place where a solution would be found. Hubert Humphrey was still in the U. S. Senate after his unsuccessful bid for the presidency in 1968, and he was still in tune as ever with the rumblings of disgruntled constituents. Humphrey's persistent prodding of the Forest Service apparently forced the agency to reconsider its position. In November, 1975, the snowmobile ban was postponed for two years. However, the reprieve was brief.

Spring came, hearings were held, and in September Butz reinstated the initial ban.

Snowmobile groups immediately filed suit in federal court. But federal judge, Donald Alsop, quickly disposed of the matter, ruling that Butz's action was well within the secretary's discretionary authority permitted by law.

There Ought to be a Law

By the spring of 1975, it was becoming increasingly apparent that a legislative showdown on the wilderness issues was unavoidable. James Oberstar, Blatnik's successor, was not eager to begin his congressional tenure on such a volatile note; however, with the protest from his eighth district swelling, the inevitable could not be ignored. Oberstar thought that a compromise was still possible. Quickly, the freshman congressman moved to neutralize the growing hostility between north and south. During the summer, he and his staff held extensive meetings with all factions in the dispute. By autumn Oberstar was ready to unveil a solution. As he explained at the time, his legislative draft had been constructed to balance the wants of wilderness advocates against "those who prefer wider recreational opportunities, and those whose livelihood depend on the area."

Preservationists, who were in no mood to surrender any of their hard fought gains, reeled in indignation. To them, Oberstar's proposal was far worse than the Forest Service's much disputed management plan. Most unacceptable was a provision in the legislative draft which would have combined 40 percent of the BWCA with another 122,700 acres bordering the canoe country. Together, the two areas would be designated as a national recreation area, permitting motorboating, snowmobiling and logging indefinitely.

Preservationists charged Oberstar with declassifying the wilderness, the ultimate heresy. The congressman retorted that his plan only officially confirmed what already existed. (The 412,000 acre Portal Zone which Oberstar's bill would have removed from the BWCA had been traditionally managed under multiple-use practices. It was here, however, where the virgin forest stood and the battle over logging was most intense.)

In an attempt to reconcile their differences, Heinselman and Dayton met several times with Oberstar and his staff. But early on, it was evident neither side intended to budge. For Oberstar, the BWCA was large enough to accommodate a range of uses; for Heinselman and Dayton, the Boundary Waters was the only canoe country in the entire fifteen million acre Wilderness System and that alone justified its preservation as wilderness in perpetuity. By mid-winter, 1976, the talks ended, and both sides fortified themselves for a long and arduous campaign.

Preservationists scrambled to protect their gains. In June, 1976, the Friends of the Boundary Waters Wilderness was founded. Headed by Bud Heinselman, the *ad hoc* group's sole purpose was to secure legislation that would preserve the BWCA "for all time as wilderness." Unlike MPIRG, the Friends had an able cadre of veterans seasoned by past environmental skirmishes. Yet, more was required. The wilderness advocates needed a congressional champion.

With Oberstar clearly allying himself with his northeastern constituents, the Friends looked south. Heinselman approached Representation Donald Fraser, a Minneapolis congressman, with an impassioned appeal for support. The congressman was sympathetic to the Friend's position on the wilderness controversy, and he believed the preservationists deserved a hearing in the halls of Congress. He was, however, hesitant to enter the fray as a legislative sponsor. After all, the BWCA was in James Oberstar's district, and certain unwritten rules discouraged the meddlesome intrusion by a House member into the in-district prerogatives of another. For this reason, Fraser felt that his direct involvement in the wilderness fight might do the cause more harm than good.

Still, Heinselman persisted in his pursuit of Fraser's sponsorship of a strong BWCA bill. Finally, his efforts bore fruit. On June 27, 1976, in the matter-of-fact manner which typified his political style, Fraser announced that he would sponsor legislation to end logging, mining, and all forms of motorized recreational use. The stage was set and the combatants were armed. The political bloodletting was about to begin.

As the two sides jockeyed for support, the court again snatched caution from the wind. Although the Eighth Circuit Court of Appeals had initially upheld Judge Lord's ruling that an environmental impact statement was required for the BWCA timber contracts, the Court was not as understanding the second time around. The appellate court stated that Lord had overstepped his judicial bounds in his latest decision. He had the right neither to substitute his judgment for that of the Forest Service's on the adequacy of the impact statement, nor to render a sweeping decree *a la* Neville on the inviolable sanctity of virgin forest. On the latter, the court of appeals submitted, "It is undisputed that some commercial logging in the BWCA was contemplated by Congress."

The appellate court's ruling was an unexpected hitch in the Friend's plans. Clearly, the virgin forest could now be cut. If the contract options were exercised, the legislative effort would be for nothing, at least as far as the forest was concerned. Only one course remained: an old-fashion appeal to fair play.

It appeared certain that Congress would enact some form of BWCA legislation during its coming session, permanently settling the logging dispute, one way or another. If the companies holding BWCA timber contracts voluntarily refrained from executing them now, future logging – if permitted by Congress – would have the full force of law behind it and, of course, result in less public criticism, too. Environmentalists prayed that this argument would work.

The Friends found an unlikely emissary to carry their adjuration to the timber companies, Eighth District Congressman James Oberstar. Both personally and politically, Oberstar favored a multiple-use management approach for the BWCA. Yet, restraint now seemed a politically prudent course. Oberstar feared that logging in the BWCA during the congressional hearings on his bill could only inflame an already emotionally charged climate. This would make his task even more difficult.

Oberstar met with timber company representatives and a delay resulted. The concession brought a deep sigh of relief from nervous preservationists, but the pause was brief. With the fate of the virgin forest hanging precariously on the momentary good will of those who would destroy it, the preservationists intensified their efforts to remove BWCA logging from the law. As John Blatnik's top aide for twelve years, James Oberstar had learned the lessons of legislative politics, and the congressman knew he was at a decided disadvantage. The Friends were mobilizing national support for Fraser's bill, and he realized that an unsavory pro-business tag would be placed on his legislation. Oberstar had to show that the average, working American would be harmed by Fraser's bill.

To convey this message, a grass roots effort was essential. Oberstar presented the strategy to his disgruntled constituents, and they responded enthusiastically. In May, 1977, the Boundary Waters Conservation Alliance was formed. From its inception, however, the Alliance was beset with an ineptness wrought of political *naïveté*. The northlanders were a forthright people, believing that right is right and would prevail in the end. This credo worked perfectly well in their daily lives, and most saw no reason why it would not work equally well in their current endeavor. After all, they were the people who, over the years, had yielded much for the wilderness's benefit. In the past, they had seen, though grudgingly at times, a reason for their concessions. And in the process a balance had been struck which considered the needs of all. But now, it seemed to them, a small group of wilderness purists wanted everything while offering nothing in return. This was clearly dogma, not reason; pernicious dictates rather than conciliatory compromise. All that was needed was to spread the truth, and the North Country would surely be vindicated – again, right would prevail.

As events unfolded, the Alliance discovered that the right is seldom the basis for political success. Throughout the travail, the Alliance's leadership appeared ill-at-ease with the media. Suspicion of the media's bias was reinforced by disparaging news stories which quoted local residents making curt and sometimes inflammatory remarks. Furthermore, press releases intending to clarify the Alliance's position on the competing bills seemed never to appear in print exactly as issued. When out of frustration the Alliance leadership finally attacked the media, predictably, the situation only worsened.

While tact was in short supply, the unity necessary to sustain a lengthy political fight often seemed nonexistent. Crucial decisions were normally made only after an exhausting group debate, with the loudest and most persistent voices frequently carrying the vote. Minor organizational details were laboriously discussed; contradictory pronouncements from self-appointed group spokespersons sometimes surfaced, due mainly to the lack of a clearly delineated chain-of-command. As the congressional showdown drew near, a petty dispute emerged between Alliance members in Ely and Grand Marais over the composition of the delegation which would be sent to Washington to present a final appeal. Clearly, the individuality and self-reliance so highly prized by these two North Country communities worked only, in this struggle, to sabotage their political effectiveness.

In contrast to the Alliance, the Friends of the Boundary Waters Wilderness became an effective political pressure group. Bud Heinselman, though himself a political novice, quickly developed a knack for legislative lobbying. Strategy was all important. Heinselman knew that time and the *status quo* worked to Oberstar's advantage. Success required constant pressure on Congress, the kind that could be best achieved through the mobilization of national support for Fraser's bill. The Friends therefore concluded that their first step must be a publicity blitz which would apprise wilderness enthusiasts, particularly canoeists, of the perilous situation facing the Boundary Waters.

Nearly 200,000 people visited the BWCA annually; over 70 percent were wilderness canoeists. The Forest Service issued permits to canoe country travelers and Heinselman knew that the records were on file in Duluth. With these records, a direct mailing campaign could be organized. The Forest Service, apparently wishing to appear neutral, denied the Friends access to the records. The Friends quickly followed with a freedom of information request, and the records were promptly released. Chuck Dayton later confided that although their action "infuriated the other side... it was one of the best things we did."

With the list in hand, the Friends began their mailing campaign to muster support for Fraser's bill. The effort paid handsome dividends. Letters extolling the virtues of wilderness, denigrating its callous assailants, and demanding support for Fraser's legislation flooded Congress. Congressman Phillip Burton, a liberal Democrat from San Francisco, headed the House subcommittee that was slated to conduct hearings on the BWCA legislation. Burton was a staunch pro-wilderness force in the House and was, in fact, then championing a special cause of his own – increased protection for California's coastal redwood forests.

Much of the BWCA mail eventually found its way to Burton's National Parks and Insular Affairs subcommittee office in the Longsworth House Office Building. One day, in early spring 1977, Burton passed through the narrow foyer leading to his office. Pausing briefly to leaf through some recently received mail, the congressman noticed several large boxes stacked in the corner. Asking about the contents, an aide informed Burton that the boxes contained letters concerning a canoe area in Minnesota, overwhelmingly supporting Fraser's bill. This piqued Burton's interest. What was so special about this canoe country wilderness to elicit such intense support throughout the nation, the congressman wondered. And he was to have an answer.

Over the next several months, the subcommittee chairman pushed his staff to research and brief him on every aspect of the competing BWCA bills. Both sides later agreed that Burton's acute interest in the BWCA controversy played a major role in determining the final outcome of the legislative battle.

Hearings on the two BWCA bills were scheduled for the summer of 1977. Since neither Fraser nor Oberstar were members of the parks subcommittee, and Burton himself was swamped with other legislative business, the California congressman assigned a Minnesota freshman congressman, Bruce Vento, to chair the hearings. Vento was ambivalent about the assignment. This whole wilderness business was shaping up to be one which could only blow an ill wind over an aspiring political career. Yet, if he could be instrumental in brokering a solution to this divisive controversy, the result would be an accomplishment usually reserved for a more seasoned politician. Vento decided to try.

In July, Vento, Fraser, and Oberstar headed for Minnesota to hold hearings on the bills in St. Paul and Ely. A mood of frustration and suspicion permeated the state. Most partisans felt ill-at-ease about the fate of the wilderness being decided in a place so far away, one which was notorious for its political deals emphasizing expediency over principle. But now people on both sides of the issue would have their say, and that is exactly what they intended to do.

From the start, in St. Paul, acrimony peppered the testimony of many of the speakers and angry outbursts repeatedly occurred from the audience. Scientific integrity, the aesthetic value of wilderness, the preciousness of jobs, the importance of recreational diversity and even the plight of the handicapped, who, it was claimed, would be the victims of discrimination if the Fraser bill prevailed, were themes visited and revisited as one speaker after another came forward to convey a personal and sometimes apocalyptic vision of the consequences of the competing bills.

In Ely, Heinselman found an unsettling reception awaiting him. Both he and Sigurd Olson, a long time resident of this North Country community, were hung in effigy outside the hearing meeting hall. So emotionally charged was the atmosphere inside, at one point during Olson's testimony, Vento threatened to halt the proceedings altogether if a more appropriate decorum was not immediately observed. Although the hearings provided a stage for venting deep-seated animosities which had been festering for some time, the public forum seemed only to heighten, rather than sooth the emotional climate surrounding the wilderness controversy.

Back to Canada

With the public hearings on the Fraser and Oberstar bills barely completed and the long, hot days of mid-July settling in, the wilderness affray took on a new antagonist. Like a formula soap opera, piling one unbelievable crisis upon another, Ontario revealed plans to construct an 800-megawatt, coal-fired generating plant in Atikokan, a small mining community just north of Quetico Provincial Park. The announcement brought an immediate swell of protest on both sides of the border.

Like other environmental hazards, the harmful effects of coal-fired emissions were just being fully understood. In this case, the problem begins with the burning of high sulfur coal. The sulfur in the coal reacts with oxygen during combustion to form sulfur dioxide gas. When the gas bonds with water, usually in the form of rain or snow, an acid is formed. Ominously called "acid rain," the chemical compound alters the ecological balance, particularly in lakes and streams, by lowering an ecosystems pH, or acid level. Aquatic life forms with a low tolerance to higher pH levels die or fail to reproduce. The consequences are eventually felt throughout the ecosystem's food chain. At the time, some lakes in the northeastern United States and eastern Canada were devoid of much aquatic life because of years of acid deposition from coal-fired generating plants in the Midwest. Natural systems with low buffering capacities – that is, with little alkaline material such as limestone – were particularly sensitive to the more acute effects of acid deposition. And the lakes in the Quetico-Superior wilderness fell perfectly into this category.

Environmentalist criticized both the size and location of the plant and the absence in the design plan of emission abatement equipment to remove the sulfurous pollutants formed during combustion. Ontario Hydro, the government sponsored energy corporation who had proposed the plan, vigorously defended the plant. Citing provisions in the plan, the energy company pointed out that the design specifications called for the use of low-sulfur, Canadian coal as fuel and the installation of 650 foot emissions stacks to disperse and dilute any harmful gas. Furthermore, the company maintained that the prevailing winds into the region came from the south and west and would blow most of the emissions away from the wilderness.

Ontario Hydro's reassurances did little to satisfy environmentalists' concerns. In an August editorial, the Minneapolis Star charged that the plant was simply "the brain child of politics" serving only to buoy the economy of a dying town. The plant's scheduled completion date in 1980 conveniently dove-tailed with the announced closing date for Atikokan's two iron ore mines. In addition, although Ontario Hydro justified the plant based on an anticipated future energy shortage, this claim was placed in doubt when the press revealed that Manitoba, a neighboring province to the west, was producing an electrical surplus which was being exported to both Ontario and the United States.

Despite the serious environmental questions raised about the plant, many Canadians continued to support its construction. The plant's economic impact for the community was clear. As invectives flowed north, resentment grew in Atikokan over American intrusion into their affairs. The plant's fate seemed to have become as much a symbol of independence as an economic necessity. Atikokan mayor, Jack Pierce, drove to the heart of the matter when he told a reporter, "Most of the opposition to this plant comes from Americans living in Canada who think they are the saviors of us Canadians. That sits raw with us." Pierce probably didn't help his cause when he added tartly, "You have to dump the stuff someplace, your backyard or ours."

Actually, the Canadians offered a point that Americans would have sooner ignored. Acid rain was a big problem in Canada, and the source of the problem was the United States. With prevailing winds coming from the south and coal-fired generating plants scattered throughout the American Midwest, eastern Canada had borne the brunt of the harmful effects from acid deposition. Meanwhile, government policy makers in the United States had consistently turned a blind eye to Canadian protestation about the problem. In Minnesota alone, thirty coal-fired facilities dotted the state – a fact Pierce was quick to point out – and released their emissions into winds which ultimately passed over the canoe country wilderness. "Is it right," questioned the Atikokan mayor, "that we Canadians should be penalized for a problem which is mainly one of your own creation?"

For some time, Canada and the United States had formally discussed a variety of mutually vexing environmental issues. The Atikokan power plant now became a small part of this bilateral conversation.

The United States State Department pressed the Environmental Protection Agency to complete a study on the plant's emission hazards. EPA's busiest field office, Region V headquartered in Chicago, got the assignment. A quickly prepared report appeared to verify the conclusions reached in Ontario Hydro's own environmental assessment: the effect of sulfur dioxide emissions would be negligible, exceeding pollution standards only two days a year.

Environmentalists, however, remained unconvinced, and with the assistance Representative Oberstar, demanded a reevaluation of the report. Grudgingly, the agency complied.

The second study was conducted closer to home at the EPA Environmental Research Laboratory in Duluth, Minnesota. Dr. Gary Glass, the project director, had been tracking the progress of acid rain research for several years and knew that major flaws existed in the initial study. He was determined to avoid those same mistakes, a resolve he was to find to be easier said than done.

Following standard research procedures, Glass's team meticulously collected snow melt and lake water samples, and they designed an intricate cybernetic model to evaluate the data. With the project running ahead of schedule, Glass's study ran into an unanticipated detour. Ontario Hydro announced that the plant would be reduced in size to 400 megawatts, one-half its original size. The size reduction also significantly altered the projected emissions, requiring the EPA researchers to adjust their model and rework all of their calculations. Then, several months before their report's completion and in the final days of the legislative contest, an EPA official in Washington again pronounced the Atikokan plant safe. That announcement was both premature and inaccurate.

Glass's report was released in draft form several months after the BWCA legislation had been signed into law. Its findings were sobering. Air quality, some terrestrial plant communities, and most aquatic animal and plant life would be adversely affected by the plant's sulfur emissions. Wrote the researchers, "As more lakes are eventually impacted, the whole philosophy behind the wilderness experience will be violated and the part of the BWCA which provides recreation will be reduced....Few people who utilized the [wilderness] could be expected to enjoy areas made fishless by pollution from human activity."

The report, however, failed to lay the matter to rest. Ontario Hydro continued to insist on the accuracy of its original study and seemed determined to press on with the project. Although a small group of local environmentalists opposed the plant's construction, most Atikokan residents favored the utility company's decision. In the States, the conflicting EPA studies and pronouncements had created confusion over the plant's ultimate environmental impact on the canoe country. As if this were not enough, claims surfaced that the State Department had used the fate of the canoe country as fodder to gain more favorable settlements on other issues in the two country's bilateral talks. Why else, some asked, would there have been such a quick, initial rush to judgment on the plant's safety?

The power plant controversy had surfaced at the same time that the Ministry of Natural Resources announced the completion of its six-year Quetico Provincial Park study. Given the troubling conclusions in Glass's report, it seemed ironic that the provincial agency adopted a new park classification system which gave full wilderness protection to the Quetico and two other primitive canoe areas. Logging, mining and mechanized recreation would be henceforth barred from the wilderness. Even fire management procedures were sharply modified, with the master plan acknowledging that "fire is the major tool which could be used to approximate a natural forest and thereby natural wildlife habitat conditions."

Since the submission of the Advisory Committee's recommendations in 1972, the process had progressed methodically; although, at times bogged down by bureaucratic inertia, Ontario's political machinery had proceeded to an orderly and thorough completion of its task. Litigation, legislation, and the strident voice of dissent were noticeably absent north of the border. Two countries, seemingly so similar in heritage and close in political goals, faced a common problem, only to adopt for its solution methods which were so different in both kind and manner. The contrast was indeed a curious one.

To Cliff McIntosh, vice-chairman of the 1971 Quetico Provincial Park Advisory Committee and president of the Quetico Center, a residential continuing education facility east of Atikokan, the riddle seemed not at all odd. "America was born through a revolutionary process, had a violent frontier, and tended to develop institutions that are adversary in nature," explained McIntoch in a letter. "Canada's origins were evolutionary, our frontiers were – and still are – peaceful, and our institutions tend to emphasize compromise and cooperation as a means of problem solving...Confrontation is far more a part of the United States' culture than it is in Canada." McIntosh's insight may have been disputed by some, yet the fact remains that substantial differences did exist, and those differences significantly colored the tone of the debate and the feelings which were left in its wake.

In Search of a Solution

The combined elation and alarm over the Quetico Park Master Plan and the proposed Atikokan power plant caused environmentalists in the United States to push even harder for a favorable legislative solution to this increasingly perplexing problem. In September 1977, spirits in the environmental community were lifted when the Carter Administration threw its weight behind a more restrictive wilderness approach to resolving the BWCA controversy. President Carter, who had campaigned on a little noticed pro-wilderness platform plank, appointed Dr. Rupert Cutler assistant agriculture secretary. A former Wilderness Society officer, Cutler's wilderness stance was no secret, and he had been given free reign by his boss, Agriculture Secretary Robert Bergland, to develop the Administration's policy in this area. Although Cutler never gave a *carte blanche* endorsement to the Fraser bill, offering instead a substitute measure, the alternative legislation closely mirrored that of the Minneapolis congressman's.

Except for the September announcement, the autumn and most of the winter was fairly calm. Burton was still busy doing his wilderness homework and his subcommittee was preoccupied with more pressing business. Besides Burton's redwood legislation, the subcommittee was handling the Omnibus Parks bill, eventually to become the largest national parks' law in history. For both sides the lull was agonizing.

By the beginning of 1978, Representatives James Oberstar and Donald Fraser had narrowed much of the gulf which had initially existed between their legislative positions. Oberstar had abandoned his national recreation area scheme, thus conceding all logging in the BWCA; Fraser had shown willingness to compromise on the motorboat issue. A middle ground finally seemed available. Yet, enmity between north and south had risen to a point where an outlet was needed to vent the building pressure. With Congress for the moment preoccupied with other matters, the media became the next best field for combat.

The Twin Cities papers, both in print and picture, repeatedly assailed James Oberstar, occasionally depicting him as an insensitive and implacable ogre who was determined to decimate the wilderness. One cartoon showed the ignoble congressman gleefully towering over a stand of recently cut trees, as all of the motorized implements so repugnant to the wilderness purists invaded the once pristine conquest. Papers in the North Country responded with a vengeance. Typical, was a cartoon of an alligator, which closely resembled the once revered Uncle Sam, voraciously gobbling up massive tracts of private land. Articles focused on the most divisive aspects of the controversy, and editorials chided one side or the other for its uncompromising and insensitive position. Letters, too, deluged the papers. Most issued sharp attacks at their opponents while proclaiming the pure intentions behind their own misunderstood and often maligned stance.

All and all, things had degenerated into a war of harsh accusations which distorted the real closeness that existed between the two sides. This period was the most emotionally rending and least purposeful episode in the whole ordeal. The bellicose climate set a tone which would persist through the remaining days of the legislative struggle.

Phil Burton recognized the staggering complexities in the BWCA affair and had mandated his subcommittee staff, with the assistance of Vento's office, to construct a compromise bill. By March, 1978, with the completed bill, Burton acted decisively, tipping the scales firmly in the preservationist's favor.

The Vento-Burton bill, as it came to be known, centered on the motorboat issue, since by then Oberstar was willing to concede logging and mining for an acceptable compromise on motorboats. But this the bill did not offer. Unlike Oberstar's initial proposal which sanctioned their use on 124 lakes, the Vento-Burton bill permitted them on only eleven lakes and one river in the BWCA. Instead of 61 percent of the water surface area opened to motorboats under Oberstar's plan, the subcommittee bill contracted that area to sixteen percent. To off-set the adverse economic impact from the logging and mining ban and the restrictions on motorboat use, the bill authorized the Forest Service to purchase resorts bordering the wilderness and expand its forest management program in the rest of Superior National Forest. The latter was primarily a job creation measure for the economically depressed region of northeastern Minnesota.

It was, however, an idea borrowed from Oberstar that raised the dander of the north wood's residents. The

Vento-Burton bill included a national recreation area but, unlike Oberstar's initial proposal, this NRA was to be carved from 227,000 acres of land outside the BWCA. The bill's proposed NRA included three road access corridors to the wilderness, and on these roads sat many resorts, homes and summer cabins. Although the bill allowed private land ownership to continue within the NRA, the area was to be subjected to a new land zoning authority administered by the secretary of agriculture. North wood's residents reeled at the thought of more federal control over their affairs. The voice of protest again rose in the north. Thoughts drifted back to the early 1950's and the land condemnation authority exercised by the Forest Service under the Thye-Blatnik Act. Once again, many feared, big brother was flexing his greedy hand.

Actually, the zoning authority given to the secretary of agriculture in the Burton bill was not as threatening as it first appeared. Burton's staff had modeled the bill's zoning provision after the Sawtooth Formula, a procedure first used in the Sawtooth National Recreation Area in Idaho. In the bill, the secretary was permitted to establish land-use codes for the recreation area. Special deference, however, was extended to existing uses, thus ensuring that no individual would be denied a use derived from his property prior to the area's change in status. Furthermore, the condemnation of private property could only occur when a code was flagrantly violated. All seemed quite harmless. Yet, fear rarely is rational, and so it was in northeastern Minnesota in the spring of 1978.

With sabers again rattling in the north, Oberstar decided to launch a final assault on the pro-wilderness bill.

As he saw it, the Vento-Burton "compromise" conveniently ignored a fundamental feature of the controversy. "These resorts and outfitters are not multi-million dollar corporations making large sums of money," the congressman wrote in a letter published in the Twin Cities papers. "These small businesses are individually owned, family-operated enterprises. Compromise is a misnomer for this legislation. The mutual give and take required in any compromise is missing. This bill sacrifices certain basic rights of the people of northern Minnesota to the interests of wilderness advocates."

Oberstar's effort was partially successful. The NRA was eventually dropped from the bill. This concession, however, was all he was to get in the House.

In early April, the parks subcommittee sent the Vento-Burton bill to the full committee. Final hearings were scheduled to begin immediately. Oberstar objected, characterizing the tactic as a "Pearl Harbor attack on northern Minnesota." Fearing that the steamrollering charge might jeopardize the bill's chances for passage, its sponsors delayed the hearings.

Wilderness Politics
Become State Politics

It was here, with the House ready to act, that legislative and electoral politics became inseparably entwined, a condition that persisted for the duration of the struggle. Minnesotans faced an unusual situation in the November election: two senate seats were up for election.

Normally, a state's senatorial elections are staggered over even-year general elections. Beginning, however, in 1976, a sequence of events unfolded that temporarily changed this practice in Minnesota. First the sitting senior senator, Walter Mondale, quit the Senate to become President Jimmy Carter's vice-president. Minnesota Governor Wendell Anderson resigned his gubernatorial office and was promptly appointed by his successor to complete the two remaining years of Mondale's term. Then, little more than one year later, Senator Hubert Humphrey died of cancer. Governor Tony Perpich, Anderson's successor, tapped the deceased senator's wife, Muriel, to fill the senatorial post until a permanent replacement could be selected in the upcoming fall election.

Donald Fraser, no longer spearheading the wilderness fight in the House, wanted Humphrey's Senate seat, while Wendell Anderson planned to seek election in his own right. And it was Anderson who held the trump card for the BWCA legislation in the Senate.

Both the Friends and the Alliance sought the senator's support for some time, yet, Anderson had remained cautiously silent on the matter. Now, with the house poised to act on Burton's bill, Anderson knew that he could no longer ignore the troublesome issue. In April, at a fundraising rally in the northeastern Minnesota community of Virginia, the senator broke his silence. There, on the doorstep of the wilderness, Anderson cast his lot with his north woods constituents. To an enthusiastic crowd, Anderson proclaimed, "This is not a fight of environmentalists vs. mining or logging. It is a fight between canoers and folks."

Anderson's announcement took wilderness advocates by surprise. Until his Virginia declaration, they had been confident that their appeals to the senator would ultimately entice his support.

Hardest hit by the unexpected development was Bud Heinselman. More than anyone, Heinselman embodied the fervor and dedication of the preservationists' cause. With seemingly inexhaustible endurance, the former Forest Service researcher had spent much of the previous year in Washington soliciting support for a pro-wilderness bill. By spring, with the House appearing ready to pass the Vinto-Burton bill, his persistence had seemed to pay off. But then came Anderson's announcement. At this point, a major set back was more than Heinselman could gracefully handle. Not prone to mince words, Heinselman charged the senator with "sticking a knife" in the BWCA legislation "to salvage his crumbling political career." (At the time, Anderson was fairing poorly in the polls, a situation which was to worsen as the legislative battle dragged on.)

With the House still uncommitted on the BWCA legislation, and Anderson and Heinselman quarreling, the Minnesota Democrat-Farmer-Labor Party (DLF) – the state arm of the national Democratic Party – met in mid-May to write its platform and endorse candidates for the fall election. The convention was tumultuous from the start. Many delegates came to the convention with rigid feelings about Fraser and Anderson and their respective BWCA positions. At one point during Donald Fraser's address to the convention, loud and continuous jeers emerged from angry northeastern Minnesota delegates. The embarrassing display was so disorderly James Oberstar had to silence the rancor before Fraser could finish his speech. Still, both Fraser and Anderson secured the endorsements: yet, the unity required for success in November was critically absent.

The Republicans were quick to capitalize on the volatile wilderness issue. David Durenberger, who would oppose Fraser for Humphrey's seat, supported the north, while Anderson's opponent, Rudy Boschwitz, sided with the preservationists. As for the party, pure pragmatism carried the day. Republican platform declared the Vento-Burton bill unacceptable. As one northeastern Minnesota delegate warned in opposing a motion that would have placed the party behind the pro-wilderness bill, "There are 50,000 swing votes in the area for the Republican candidate. Let's not sell out to a liberal faction that wouldn't vote for us even if we gave them everything."

Back in Washington, the House was ready to act. Clearing committee with only a slight change – a less irritating mining protection area replaced the controversial

National Recreation Area – the Vento-Burton bill was scheduled for a floor vote on June 5th. Approval was overwhelming: 324 for, 29 against. A major hurdle had been cleared, and it was now on to the Senate. But the Senate would have to wait in the wings a bit longer before it could claim center stage.

During the summer of 1978, press attention shifted to northeastern Minnesota. Replete with sizzling quotes and defiant acts, and capped off with Washington's version of the Great Armada, Ely was the ideal place to find a good story.

Reporters from major newspapers on both coasts descended on this slow-moving community, quickly making their rounds from shop to resort to secure, it appeared to the locals, a fervid remark or two to embellish a seemingly pre-written story. "The press blew the whole thing out of proportion," contended Bob Cary, owner, editor, and sometimes sole reporter for the Ely Echo, the town's main newspaper. "It was really a struggle of private interest versus private interest. These guys from the press who were unfamiliar with the area just couldn't, or didn't want to see it like that. Hell, they were popping in and out of here all summer wanting an inflammatory quote or a picture of the effigy hangings of Heinselman and Olson during the hearings.' With a chuckle, Cary added, "Needless to say, I went fishing a lot that summer."

The controversy attracted minor celebrity, too. Jack Ford, the son of the former president, visited Ely that summer. Ford brought with him a camera crew to film a spot illustrating the unmatched solitude one could glean from a wilderness experience. Paradoxically, much of the footage taken of Ford in his canoe was shot from the stern of a motorboat.

It was, however, outright defiance which most piqued the press's interest. Here conflict could be shown at its best. Apparently out of frustration and anger, a group of Alliance members blocked several access roads leading to BWCA departure points. Finding a road blocked by two pickup trucks and several picketing north woods residents, one annoyed canoeist complained, "Our vacations are ruined." In response an angry local shouted, "Our lives are rather ruined."

A Minneapolis newspaper promptly reported the curt exchange and two weeks later Time Magazine printed it again in a one page account of the ongoing controversy. Although this confrontation characterized a struggle which was becoming increasingly vitriolic, it also left the inaccurate impression that a permanent state of war existed on the populated borders of this canoe country wilderness.

Interestingly, the media failed to report a tactical problem faced by the local activists. The blockage of access points also hampered vacationers who wanted to patronize resorts owned by Alliance members. The barrier was, therefore, removed after only one day.

Senator Wendell Anderson found himself in a difficult political predicament. Any advantage he had gained by supporting the north had been offset by the wholesale erosion of support from environmentalists. The polls showed Anderson trailing his Republican rival, Rudy Boschwitz, particularly in the Twin Cities. But the BWCA issue was not Anderson's only problem. Questions persisted about his unorthodox move to the Senate and his general fitness for office, the latter a product of his perceived unwillingness to take a firm position on difficult legislative issues. Yet, so long as the wilderness clash persisted, Anderson's ability to counter his critics on these other issues remained greatly hindered. The wilderness issue had to be rapidly neutralized, and this required crafting a compromise which would be acceptable to everyone concerned. If he could mediate such a compromise, the issue would not only be defused, but he might emerge from this political morass as a saving hero, the master politician who from chaos wrought order by skillfully practicing "the art of the possible." This became his strategy.

The Deal

Despite the previous summer's congressional hearings and the extensive time and effort devoted to the issue by James Oberstar, northeastern Minnesotans felt that Congress had failed to understand their side of the dispute. The media had distorted their position, often characterizing them as mercenary and sometimes lawless rabble. Heinselman seemed to have developed an unduly cordial relationship with the powerful Mr. Burton, thus placing the congressman's impartiality into question. Finally, and most disturbingly, their efforts at lobbying Washington's lawmakers directly had often degenerated into arguments rather than reasoned discussion. Anderson knew that before any bargain could be struck the suspicion that Congress was only interested in attending to its own needs for expediency and power must first be dispelled.

With this in mind, the Minnesota senator arranged an event never before seen in Ely, Minnesota. In early July, Anderson's office announced that he, Mrs. Humphrey, and three members of the Senate Subcommittee on Parks and Recreation – the subcommittee handling his BWCA bill – would travel to northern Minnesota to investigate the situation first hand. In mid-July the two Minnesota senators along with subcommittee chairman Senator James Abourezk (D-South Dakota), and Senators Howard Metzenbaum (D-Ohio) and Dale Bumpers (D-Arkansas) accompanied by staff and press arrived at the small airport outside Ely.

Immediately, the senators and their entourage embarked on a grueling two day schedule. The first day began with a flight over myriad wilderness lakes, incidentally, conducted well below the Truman's 4000 foot airspace reservation. The air tour was followed by a vociferous, yet orderly public meeting, completing the first day's agenda.

The second day was one to behold. For those who would decide its fate, a trek into the wilderness was deemed essential. Here they were the senators and their supporting cast, motoring across pristine lakes, stopping briefly for an obligatory picture beside a canoe and partaking in a shore lunch on picturesque Seagull Lake; and all the while trying ever so hard to gain some sense of this place's special magic. No doubt, however, the day's tumult found the magic barely evident.

Heinselman and Dayton knew that the impressions formed during this trip could determine the direction taken by the senators once back in Washington. Hence, they had extracted from Abourezk a commitment to hear their final appeal before departing.

A tired group returned to Ely that afternoon. As they entered the meeting hall, Senator Metzenbaum pulled Dayton aside, suggesting, given the weariness of the group, that they be spared a lengthy entreaty. Dayton heeded the Ohio senator's advice, asking only that they listen to one speaker, Sig Olson. They agreed. Olson, then nearly eighty, rose and began to trace the long history of battles fought and won to preserve the sanctity of this wilderness haven. Repeatedly, the wilderness advocate and naturalist author emphasized to his distinguished audience that if previous encounters had been lost there would be no wilderness today over which to fight. The senators listened politely.

Senator Abourezk, however, had something in mind. For him the combatants were not far apart. Possibly, he thought, if he exercised the influence of his position, he could bring the dueling sides together, thus ending this painful contest once and for all. As Olson spoken, the South Dakota senator indicated that he wanted to talk to a representative from each side in this contentious dispute.

As a spokesman from each side approached, Abourezk tilting slightly in his chair, as if to impart a secret confidence, telling both men that he felt a solution close at hand and he wanted them to try once more to reach an accord. To assist in the effort, he offered a member of his staff to mediate the session. Dayton later recalled that each sides felt the other unreasonable, and that little could be gained from what had been attempted several times before. Yet, he added, when you are approached in that manner "you don't tell a committee chairman you won't try."

The temperature was in the 90's degree on the July day the two contingencies arrived in the nation's capital. Both sides' nerves were frayed and energies depleted; neither side expressed much hope for success in the upcoming negotiation. Chuck Dayton was to negotiate for the Friends, and Ron Walls was to represent the Alliance.

As promised, a committee staffer named Tom Williams had been selected by Senator Abourezk to mediate the session. Though billed by the senator as "an experienced man in these matters," Williams had never before undertaken such an endeavor. Initially reluctant, he had finally succumbed to his boss's cajolery. A confident sort, projecting his self-assurance in both appearance and manner, Williams felt game for the challenge. Maybe he could succeed where others had failed; at any rate, he thought, it promised to be a most interesting experience.

The three men met on Thursday, July 28th in the Old Senate Office Building. The meeting proved fruitful. An atmosphere of trust and comfort from which to proceed seemed to have been established.

By midday the following day, Williams sensed that the two men were willing to negotiate in earnest. Here, during a break in the discussion, he made an important move. Williams understood the importance of personality and position so central to the political power in Washington. Leaving the small conference room during the break, Williams walked down the long hallway looking for Senator Henry Jackson (D-Washington). Jackson headed the standing committee which would handle the BWCA legislation. Williams suggested and Jackson agreed that a visit by the senator with the negotiators might prove beneficial in securing an agreement.

During the afternoon session, right on cue, Jackson entered the conference room. After meting out a few formal salutations, Jackson got to the purpose of his visit. The senator assured Dayton and Walls that the Senate took their effort seriously and that he would personally see to it that legislation would be enacted based upon what two men decided. The senator's timely visit proved effective; the two men began to talk lakes.

With the stage for resolution set, the marathon began. Saturday's meeting started early, concluding twenty-one hours later. As the negotiators' supporters sat nervously "counting the mice" outside that small meeting room, Dayton and Walls meandered lake by lake on the question of motorized access. In fact, the motor access issue was the primary topic dealt with during the three day session. By the time of the Washington negotiations, tentative agreements had been reached on the other contentious issues.

The talks ended early Sunday morning. Both sides were tired but relieved; the possible had been accomplished and ratification was all that remained. Ratification, however, was not a forgone certainty.

Back Home

When word reached Minnesota about the accord, the reaction was hardly one of elation. Neither Dayton nor Walls received a hero's welcome. Both men were criticized for their "excessive concessions." However, it was Ron Walls who received the angriest reaction.

Walls' brother had died on the eve of the talks and he had initially declined to participate in the Washington negotiations. The Alliance's leadership remained persistent in their appeal and Walls finally acquiesced. Now he was being cast as an unwitting villain in a betrayal of the first order.

From the start, the Ely attorney confronted firm and vocal opposition to the plan. First unveiled in Grand Marais, the plan was soundly rejected. News traveled fast in the North Country. By the time Walls reached Ely, a hostile atmosphere had begun to fuel its own flames. Exhausted and discouraged, Walls tried to lay out the provisions of the Washington accord to his fellow townspeople. But they would hear none of it. The critical reception, which often cut right to the core of his loyalty, hurt Walls deeply.

The criticisms were many. Why had he violated his orders? Hadn't he been instructed to agree to nothing, to sign nothing, to stonewall, and to hope for the best later? And for some he had, in no uncertain terms, sold out. For a brief moment, Walls stood before the chiding throng as a child before his scolding father, contrite and wan, yet innocently unaware of the error which had provoked such a storm of wrath in the first place. Recalling the intensity of that meeting one year later, Bob Cary recounted, "I looked at Ron and he looked back at me, and I just shrugged my shoulders. There wasn't a damn thing I could do for him."

The Alliance overwhelmingly rejected the pact. Oberstar had felt all along that the mediation session was a tactical blunder. At the time, it was rumored that the congressman had favored the rejection of the Dayton-Walls accord. Whether true or not, it was no secret that many in the Alliance voted against the agreement because they hoped that time and the status quo would continue to work to their advantage. Candidly, one member of the group professed several days later, "A majority of the Alliance now hopes that nothing will be passed this year by Congress. That's what we will be working for. That and the defeat this fall of Fraser."

As the Friends embarked on what might well have been a similar ordeal for Chuck Dayton, news of the North Country's rejection hit the media. The group's meeting was already in progress and had been experiencing some discord of its own. When the news from Ely was announced, the meeting adjourned. Voting now seemed pointless. More important was the preparation that would be necessary for the final clash to come.

For both Dayton and Walls, two men who had met as equals to parley from reason rather than dogma to find a solution through measured deliberation rather than obstinate resistance, the rebuff of their efforts marked a personal low point in this long, arduous affair.

The Fallout

Anderson was exasperated by the defeat. The Minnesota senator, who had been guardedly optimistic over the chances for success, now found himself in an awkward situation. He had a compromise brokered by the Senate and a rejection of that compromise by the very group Anderson had sworn to defend. To make matters worse, his campaign was still flagging badly. August polls showed him favored by less than forty percent of registered voters. The Senator had been desperate for a dramatic solution to this intractable controversy, and preferably a solution for which he could take credit. But now it was evident that there would be no easy, let alone heroic, exit; the issue had to be confronted head-on.

In early August, Anderson revealed that he would sponsor a bill paralleling the Dayton-Walls accord. Visibly perturbed, the senator admitted that although "it's not what I want," the bill was better for the people of the northeast than the House alternative. But many people in the northeastern Minnesota did not agree. For them, no legislation at all was preferable. This is what they sought and it was exactly what they expected their senator to deliver. Shocked by Anderson's abrupt reversal, a gale of scorn swept the North Country. "A man made a promise to us, and he reneged on that today," fired Bruce Kerfoot, an Alliance officer. It was to be Anderson's political epitaph.

Anderson's bill was introduced, only to be shoved aside as the Senate considered more important matters. August ran into September and the Minnesota primary election. Anderson faced five opponents in his primary race, winning the nomination comfortably with 57% of the vote.

Donald Fraser ran for the DFL nomination in the second Senate race. He faced a more formidable opponent. Bob Short, a millionaire businessman and several times election bridesmaid, challenged the eight term congressman for the DFL nomination for Minnesota's second senate seat. Short attacked Fraser at every turn, first in the north on the wilderness issue, and then elsewhere in the state on the congressman's liberal stance on abortion and gun control. Fraser's team found itself constantly on the defensive, repelling one stinging charge after another. For a man who had based his political career on reason and integrity, Fraser refused to surrender principle to expediency. But the campaign in its waning days was more than the embattled congressman could control. An aide close to both Fraser and his wilderness proposal later reflected, "Don never was able to take the initiative. There was no way he could given the tempo of the campaign and the kind of man he was. He just wasn't a roll-in-the-dirt campaigner."

To the last, however, the outcome remained uncertain. On the eve of the election, one poll actually showed Fraser holding a slight advantage. For Short the key to victory depended on the north and an abnormally large favorable voter turnout.

The Range, as it was called due to its seemingly inexhaustible supply of iron ore and other metals, had always been a bastion of DFL support. The North County's support for the Democratic Party was so loyal, even George McGovern, in his disastrous bid for the presidency in 1972, carried the Eighth District by 20,000 votes, while losing the state by nearly five times that margin.

Short rarely missed a bet to exploit this wedge, constantly poking at the opened wound inflicted during the wilderness battle. At one point, Short even imported professional baseball's pugnacious manager, Billy Martin, to assist his campaign. Martin, who had once managed Short's Texas Rangers ball club, wasted no time making his feelings known on a variety of subjects – one, of course, being motors in the BWCA.

True to form, a confrontation quickly ensued between Martin and the press. Martin was quoted in a Minneapolis newspaper as saying that "it would be suicide" to travel with his son in the wilderness on a windy day without a motor. When the newspaper's editorial page accused Martin of slinging a "wild pitch," Martin quickly corrected the paper's characterization, suggesting instead that his remark was a "deliberate knockdown" and not just an errant toss. Unfortunately, this was not the only knockdown attempt that Fraser had to dodge as the campaign moved to a close.

On September 12, 1978, Minnesota voters went to the polls. The following day, Fraser acknowledged defeat. He had failed by only 3,471 of nearly 520,000 votes cast. Unfortunately for the Party, the late August polls showed

Fraser holding a decided advantage over the Republican opponent, Dave Durenberger, while Short was shown losing in the same match up. Durenberger would eventually win in November.

Apparently, Short's strategy had worked. Voter turnout in the three counties encircling the BWCA was significantly higher then in the Twin Cities area. The Twin Cities' counties of Hennepin and Ramsey accounted for 37 percent of the State's 2.2 million registered voters. Those two counties, however, drew only 33 percent of its registered voters to the polls. Cook, Lake, and St. Louis counties in northeastern Minnesota brought 70 percent of its registered Democrats to the polls. Short captured nearly three quarters of that vote.

The election result buoyed the spirits of those in the north. They had defeated their chief foe; the legislation was surely next.

Donald Fraser's defeat stunned the wilderness advocates. He had been a faithful champion throughout this struggle, and, now, in spite of their active support during the campaign, he faced the prospect of political anonymity.

Mourning was brief; concern over the fate of the wilderness legislation increased, and concern was definitely warranted. How would Congress interpret Fraser's defeat? Would legislators take it as a rebuff of the more restrictive provisions included in the bill? And most worrisome, what would Anderson do now? He had changed positions once; he could certainly do it again.

Fearing the worst, the preservationists regrouped for the final push. The Ninety-fifth Congress was in its final days.

As usual, the activity was hectic on Capitol Hill. Legislators and lobbyists hurried about, dealing and cajoling, trying to expedite or delay the progress of a particular piece of legislation. Heinselman and Brock Evans, his Sierra Club ally, were no exception, deploying persuasion and their clout wherever they could.

In the House, Phil Burton had secured approval to go to conference if and when the Senate acted. (Since the Senate was considering its own version of the BWCA legislation, in the event of passage, a conference committee comprising of members of both bodies would be convened to resolve the difference in the two bills.) But by October, the BWCA legislation still languished in committee, taking a back seat to the all important Alaska National Interest Lands Conservation bill. Adjournment had been set for mid-October. The end of this legislative session was dangerously near, and many of legislators were increasingly preoccupied with their own elections back home.

Suddenly, a break came. On October 4, following a brief forty-five minute discussion, the Senate Committee on Energy and Natural Resources released the bill; five days later the legislation passed the Senate. On Thursday, October 12, one day before the scheduled end of the legislative session, the House and Senate conferees met and accepted the Senate bill *in toto.*

With time running out, success or failure depended entirely on a few precious ticks of the clock. The rules required the House to act first, since it had requested the conference. Heinselman and Evans redoubled their efforts.

Vento personally lobbied the House Speaker, Tip O'Neil, for a place on the final agenda.

Vento's persistence paid off; O'Neil agreed. The BWCA bill would be brought to a vote. Finally, the stage was set for an orderly and, hopefully, uneventful conclusion to this whole exhausting affair. However, the political history of this serene wilderness had rarely been orderly or uneventful, and the final hours of the legislative session for the BWCA bill remained true to that history.

Early Saturday morning, less than twenty-four hours before the legislative session ended, the BWCA bill was brought to the House floor. Representatives Burton and Oberstar made their final appeals, a vote was called for, and House approval was secured. It was now on to the Senate where Heinselman and Evans hoped for an equally perfunctory result.

Congressman Burton had a reputation for being fully committed to legislation that he favored. Despite the large volume of business still before the House, Burton constantly checked on the status of the wilderness bill, maintaining an open line of communication with Senator Henry Jackson. Morning passed and no bill appeared. Something was obviously wrong. Burton checked with a House clerk and discovered that the BWCA bill had been mistaken for another bill that had already passed both houses of Congress. With the error uncovered, the bill was rushed to the Senate.

That afternoon, the conference report was introduced in the Senate. Suddenly, Senator Gaylord Nelson (D-Wisconsin), usually a dependable friend of environmental legislation, rose and began speaking against the bill. Heinselman, who had been watching from the Senate gallery, exploded from his seat and tore downstairs, searching for Sierra Club lobbyist, Jonathan Ela. Ela, who at the time was attending to another matter, promptly sent a message to Nelson, requesting a meeting with the Wisconsin senator. Moments later Nelson appeared. The two men talked briefly, only to determine that the senator had been misinformed as to the Club's and Anderson's position on the legislation. With the misunderstanding corrected, Nelson ceased his objection, a vote was taken and the bill was passed. On the twenty-first of October 1978 President Jimmy Carter signed the Boundary Waters Canoe Area Wilderness bill into law. The struggle was finally over, or was it?

Public Law 95-495 dealt with the many contentious issues which had plagued this wilderness for nearly a decade. The controversial paragraph 4(d) (5) of the Wilderness Act allowing motorboat use and logging within the BWCA was repealed. Mining and logging were banned within the 1,078,698 acre wilderness area. The word Wilderness was added to the canoe country's name in order to reflect the status change conferred in the new law and the BWCAW was enlarged by an additional 48,000 acres. In addition, an approximately 222,000 acre Mining Protection Area bordering the wilderness was created to further buffer it from the adverse effects of mineral development. To offset any adverse economic impact of the legislation, federal funds were promised for an intensive forest management, outdoor recreational development, and business assistance programs.

On the question of motors, however, the preservationists fell short of their goal. Snowmobiling continued, though limited to specified routes leading to two Canadian entry points. On the issue of motorboats, the biggest concessions were made. Unlike the Vento-Burton bill, which would have virtually ended motorboating in the BWCAW, the new law, reflecting the provisions of the Dayton-Walls accord, left twenty of largest lakes – comprising 24 percent of the water surface – permanently open to motorboats. Resort owners suffering economic hardship due to the restriction on the use of motorboats could request federal purchase of their property through September, 1983.

The legislative struggle was finished, but not without cost. In November, Wendell Anderson was soundly defeated, receiving an embarrassing 41 per cent of the vote. And Anderson was not the only casualty. The 1978 election proved a disaster for the Minnesota Democrats and came to be referred to as "the Minnesota Massacre." The Republicans, in their strongest showing in twenty-four years, captured both U.S. Senate seats, won the gubernatorial race, and gained a draw in the State's House of Representatives. (In the previous legislative session the DFL held 75 percent of the seats.)

It would probably be specious to attribute the Republican landslide solely to the wilderness struggle: however, the fact remains that the stormy years of this divisive donnybrook placed the incumbents and their party at a distinct disadvantage. The voters expected their political officials to devise a solution that was acceptable to all, and those officials had failed. The fact that the task was probably impossible from the start was of little consequence when voters pulled the levers in November.

The Struggle Continues

From the start, the legislative push had been touted by preservationists as a way to end, once and for all, the controversies that had shrouded this canoe country wilderness for nearly a decade. Instead, new issues emerged, together with controversies of their own. By the spring of 1979, some of the combatants were back in court. A disgruntled faction of the Alliance, assisted this time by a new ally, the National Association of Property Owners, filed suit in federal court, claiming that the new law discriminated against the handicapped by denying them the essential motorized means necessary to partake in the wilderness experience. The suit was later expanded to contend that an environmental impact statement on the economic effects of the legislation was required by law.

The new law had, for the first time, authorized an agent of the federal government to establish regulations for the use of motors within the wilderness. Governance of the lakes, even when surrounded by federal land, had always been exclusively exercised by the State. The State filed suit challenging this

In May, 1980, Judge Miles Lord heard arguments on the two cases and by June rejected both plaintiffs' assertions, issuing a summary judgment favoring to the federal government's position on this matter. The cases were appealed and arguments were presented to the federal circuit court on June 18, 1981. The appeals also proved unsuccessful.

Problems cropped up elsewhere. In Washington, the Administration and Congress repeatedly haggled over the economic assistance called for in the BWCAW law. Although the Carter Administration pledged support for further appropriations, it submitted two budget figures far below what had been originally promised. The House Appropriations Committee twice restored the proposed funding levels, and the Senate, though moving at a pace that caused considerable consternation in northeastern Minnesota, eventually passed the House bill.

In 1981, Ronald Reagan assumed the presidency. With Reagan came his combative interior secretary, James Watt. Although the BWCAW was still managed by the Forest Service, an agency under the jurisdiction of the agriculture department, Watt's interior department controlled land purchases. The department immediately froze all new land purchases, thus stalling the implementation of the BWCAW law's resort buy-out program and creating an atmosphere of uncertainty and suspicion in the North Country. The freeze was eventually lifted, but by then the Reagan budget proposal had completely eliminated the resort buy-out funds.

Other economic components of the BWCAW law also ran into problems. Finding itself caught in a budgetary bind, the Forest Service dragged its feet on the spending for improved recreational facilities. This provision of the new law was intended to be part of an overall forest management program, having the added purpose of serving as economic stimulus for northeastern Minnesota.

The situation in Canada remained unsettled, too. In the summer of 1979, Ontario Hydro began preparing the site for the proposed power plant. Its completion date was set for 1984. And if this were not enough, the summer of 1979 saw a new player enter the ongoing drama. Atomic Energy of Canada Ltd., a government-owned company responsible for Canada's nuclear program, announced that it would conduct test drilling north of Atikokan to determine the suitability of the site as a possible dump site for radioactive waste.

Final Words

As some worked to forestall the preservationists' gains, others contemplated the day when the last motor would be forever purged from the wilderness.

During the summer of 1979, I spoke with Bud Heinselman at his Saint Paul, Minnesota home. We talked about the recent struggle and the future for the canoe country. On the subject of his group's push for a complete motor ban, Heinselman was adamant. "It was the right thing to do," he maintained. "We were just politically unrealistic, there wasn't enough support. Maybe another generation will work to that end." Then pausing slightly, he added emphatically, "In fact, I would bet on it."

Several months later I spoke with an Alliance leader, Frank Salerno by telephone about the economic impact of the BWCAW legislation on the area. He expressed a need for remedial legislation and made himself clear that he wasn't talking about a government hand out. I asked him if he expected Congress to reverse the restrictions in the new law on the use of motors in the canoe country. Exactly, he said. Considering the history of the area and its steady trend toward tighter wilderness protection, was this a realistic expectation, I asked. Yes, he responded, and then added, "People up here have been sitting tight and waiting to see what is going to happen with the court cases. If we lose those, and something isn't done about the situation, I wouldn't be surprised if you see some civil disobedience." Salerno claimed the Alliance still had 6,000 active members and said he had just returned from a packed meeting on the "BWCA problem."

Underlying the decade of turmoil was a struggle over two equally noble, yet ostensibly incompatible ideals: the sanctity of wilderness and the cherished regard for an unfettered way of life. To the wilderness faithful any contraction of the last morsels of our once vast North American wilderness was wholly unacceptable; any proposal for its use except as a time honored museum to commemorate and experience first hand this dwindling relic from the past was akin to blasphemy. But to the North Country residents – and for that matter, probably for most people living in small, rural communities belonging more to the last century than this one – any intrusion upon their perceived independent way of life was equally unacceptable; any proposal that would have them change to meet the demands of the modern age bordered on blasphemy as well.

The real irony of the Quetico-Superior struggle is that the two states most revered in the deep recesses of an individual's sanity-preserving fantasies – an independent and self-sufficient lifestyle and the setting in which this experience could be most fully realized – came in conflict, waged battle and, most sadly, appeared to stand ready to begin the feud anew.

And the hundred years' wilderness war sputtered on.

Epilogue

In the years following the passage of the *Boundary Waters Canoe Area Wilderness Act* and the corresponding administrative actions on Quetico Provincial Park, a few challenges to the new law's implementation emerged.

The initial court challenges to the Boundary Water's legislation were quickly rebuffed and the anticipated problems with the energy proposals across the boarder never materialized. Disagreement over administrative actions regarding recreational use issues continued during the 1990's, but none of these disputes threatened the core wilderness experience one would enjoy when travelling in the canoe country. By the turn of the century, matters seemed settled for this pristine wilderness.

Several months ago, a friend and fellow canoeist, Armond Spikell, sent me an article on an ongoing controversy in the canoe country. I was alarmed by what I read. The article reported efforts by Twin Metals Minnesota, a subsidiary of Chilean business conglomerate named Antofagasta, to reacquire mineral leases for land within a watershed that flowed through the Boundary Waters.

I had been aware of this threat but had understood that it had been neutralized when the Obama Administration had effectively blocked the mining plan by declining to renew those mineral leases. Then the Trump Administration's Interior Department indicated that the Obama decision would be reexamined. To no one's surprise, in December 2018 the federal government announced its intention to renew Twin Metals' mineral leases following a 30 day review process. A Department spokesman is quoted in the article as saying that the new administration was "working to rectify 'a flawed decision rushed out the door' before Mr. Trump took office."

Since the 2016 election, Twin Metals Minnesota had been actively advancing its effort to secure and renew the suspended leases and to begin the development of its cooper-nickel mining operation. These leases involve the same mineral rights that were held by INCO in 1973.

Twin Metals' original waste disposal plan involved a water transport system between the Rainy River and the Great Lakes basins. Because of the Great Lakes Compact, which establishes rules on water use from Lake Superior, the company feared that the plan's approval would not be forthcoming. A traditional water dam system of waste containment was not politically viable. As a result Twin Metals changed its waste containment plan to one that employed a dry-stacked tailings storage facility. Both the anticipated approval difficult of the initial waste plan and the desire to reduce concerns over possible water contamination in the BWCAW from the mine's activity, accounted for this change. And in August 2019, Twin Metals, committing itself to use only union workers in the construction phase of the project, signed an agreement with local unions. As things stand now, the development plan appears real.

Twin Metals' mining proposal has been opposed by environmental groups, who are concerned about the possible degradation of the outdoors' recreational amenities in the region. In June 2019, a group composed of both environmental and local business interests filed suit seeking to overturn the reinstatement of Twin Metals' leases.

The State of Minnesota has also waded deeper into this controversy. With concern over the Trump Administration's curtailment of the federal environmental review process, Minnesota's Department of Natural Resources announced in November of 2019 that it would conduct an independent environmental review of the proposed mine.

Meanwhile, a second copper-nickel mining proposal is ongoing near the North Country town of Babbitt, just south of Ely. Both mines will be in a geological formation called the Duluth Complex. Although outside the BWCAW's watershed, concern exists over the impact of the sulfur component in the cooper ore deposits and the potential impact on both ground water and nearby water ways. PolyMet Mining, the project's owner, has acquired all of the permits necessary to begin construction. Currently, those permits are being challenged in both state and federal courts.

A controversy over mining sparked the beginning of a ten year struggle that resulted in full wilderness protection for this precious canoe country. It is sadly coincidental that another mining threat has emerged nearly one hundred years after the first efforts to protect this lake land wilderness from development. Perhaps Chuck Dayton was more prescient than he realized when in 1979 he characterized the fight he had led as only a small part of a hundred years' war.

As I approach my seventy-fifth birthday, I have become increasingly aware of how places like the Quetico-Superior wilderness have enriched my life. As a young man following my first wilderness experience, I purchased a recently published Sierra Club book authored by two brothers, Terry and Renny Russell. In authoring this book, they intended to convey their deeply personal feelings about wilderness. At one point they wrote, "We've learned to take care of ourselves where it really matters. The next step is to take care of the *places* that really matter."

It is this sentiment coupled with the Boundary Waters' current threat that prompted me to self-publish this story of protection. Regardless of how this mining controversy plays itself out, I hope that by telling this story, my effort will serve as a reminder that this special place exists today because others fought the battles necessary to save it from development. At some point, it may fall to each of us to continue this fight. At some point, action may be required. If at first you are tempted to ignore this call, I suggest that you consider a thought Edward Abbey provided on such a choice: "Sentiment without action is the ruin of the soul."

THE END

Notes:

All direct quotes are taken from interviews, official documents or transcripts, and quotation attribution appearing in newspaper articles published in the Minneapolis Tribune.

The following individuals granted me interviews or provided a written responds to my correspondence (Bold print indicates the latter.): **John Anderson**, Cliff Ahlgren, **Edmund C. Bray, Larry Beresford,** Bob Cary, Arron Klemz, Charles K. Dayton, Brock Evans, Gary Glass, Ray Haik, Miron L. Heinselman, Jody Kauchick, **Clifford McIntosh**, John O'Connor, Phillip Olfelt, Jack Pierce, Rip Rapson, Dean Rebuffoni, Frank Salerno, **R. J. Vrancart,** Thomas B. Williams, Ferguson Wilson, **T. Alan Wolten** and Edward Zabinsky. **Bold print indicates written correspondence.** (Ron Walls would not speak with me when I first approached him in 1980. I was in Ely every summer through 1995. I regret not making a greater effort to engage him in a conversation about his role in this matter.)

I used R. Newell Searle's *Saving Quetico-Superior: A Land Set Apart* extensively and Grace Lee Nute's *The Voyageur* for the Crucial Years portion of this story. I highly recommend both books for anyone wishing to read more about Quetico-Superior's earlier history and efforts made to save this wilderness from development. I found the journalistic coverage of this conflict by the Minneapolis Tribune indispensable. The public documents examine where transcripts of the federal logging and mining trials and the resulting judicial decisions, and the Quetico Provincial Park hearings transcripts housed in Toronto. Other public documents reviewed were the *Wilderness Preservation Act* and the *Boundary Waters Canoe Area Wilderness Act* and the EPA study done in Duluth on the impact of air pollutants on the canoe country. *Boundary Waters Wilderness Ecosystem* was an occasional reference for understanding certain natural features of the area. In addition, I examined several advocacy group publications in the process of preparing this manuscript. Finally, the quote on page 109 is from an article in the New York Times by Hiroko Tabuchi and Steve Eder on June 25, 2019.

I make no claim that this is an exhaustive rendering of all the facts surrounding this struggle. It is, however, a fair representation of the flow of this struggle, capturing the enormous effort made by many to protect this wilderness for the enjoyment of people today. Furthermore, I hope that my project is concise and true enough to attract the attention of Quetico-Superior's natural constituency. No fight is ever permanently won. Continued vigilance for those things that we hold most dear is forever required. Although my days of travelling the canoe country have passed, my memory of moments in this special wilderness are both vivid and deeply satisfying. Finally, my primary purpose for engaging this topic is clearly stated in the final two pages of this story.

THREE ESSAYS

The Portage

I pulled into the strip mall at the corner of Main and Whip in Centerville, Ohio. As I slowed to a stop, I could hear the gray slush slap against the bottom of my van. It was late March and the chill in the air suggested that winter was not about to relinquish its hold easily this year. As I entered the small outdoor equipment store, Wilderness Outfitters, I was greeted by the store manager and wilderness traveling companion, Matt Turton

"Hey, how're the canoe trips shaping up?" Matt asked.

"Not bad," I replied. "They're both filled already."

"Great! How do they look? Can they handle the challenge?" He asked with knowing smile.

"I think so. They look like a pretty spirited bunch."

"They better be," Matt said emphatically, laughing as he continued to stock new merchandise.

Matt is an experienced canoeist. In fact, his wilderness baptism had occurred several years earlier on a trip I ran with my business partner, Jim Rowley. Turton, like many of our young neophytes, had signed on for what he expected to be a marvelous fishing expedition. The fishing was good on Matt's trip, but he and his companion quickly discovered that there is a bit more to a wilderness canoe trip than mere angling ecstasy.

As I drove away from the store, I pictured Matt's cryptic smile, and I knew exactly what it concealed. Hidden behind his smile was an awareness of an understanding of one's self that many of our young canoeists gain on a wilderness trip like ours. My opportunity to be a part of this revelatory experience is the main reason I continue running canoe trips in the Quetico-Superior wilderness.

Quetico-Superior is a companion lake land wilderness located in northeastern Minnesota and northwestern Ontario. Officially designated the Boundary Waters Canoe Area Wilderness in the United States and Quetico Provincial Park in Canada, this roughly two million acre wilderness is today much as it was 300 years ago when the first Europeans dipped the red blades of their paddles into the clear, cold water of these glacially-carved lakes. The maze of interlocking lakes in the Quetico-Superior makes this wilderness ideal for flat-water canoe travel. Although short rivers connect the lakes, dead-fall, heavy vegetation and the rivers' rough granite beds render most unnavigable. And even when open, the water often flows too fast and is too shallow to be safely run in a canoe. Consequently, the canoeists must pass from lake to lake over a land trail called a portage, a name appropriately derived from a French word meaning to carry. It is here, on the portage, that our young canoeists' understanding is poignantly cultivated – or rather I should say, harshly imposed.

Most of the area's portages were first created by large animals such as moose and bears wandering about this wilderness in search of food and mates. Seeking the least line of resistance, these animals blazed their trails along the low lying cuts and folds in this rugged, undulating land.

Fortunately, man subdued his penchant for complicating even the simplest task and followed the animals' lead. Even so, the task that awaits the canoeist who travels through this region still requires considerable effort.

The first Europeans to enter the Quetico-Superior region were well equipped for the challenges that this wilderness imposed. Standing on average five feet six inches tall and frequently possessing a disproportionately large, muscular upper body, these hardy Frenchmen roamed the vast North American wilderness long before their better known frontier counterparts to the south were even born. They called themselves voyageurs, a title they claimed with a fierce sense of pride and savored the physical and austere life their vocation required.

Like the cowboy in the American west, the voyageur is the romantic legacy of the Quetico-Superior region. The tales of their exploits are fortunately preserved in the journals of those who traveled the interior of the North American continent under their guidance and protection. And not surprisingly, one undertaking was described in considerable detail and with equal reverence: the portage. While reading these accounts today, one can easily picture this eighteenth century fellow lugging his heavy load across a portage trail. He would carry at least two ninety pound packs of gear or furs in a single crossing. And this demanding task was often performed many times during a day that could include twelve to fifteen hours of paddling.

The bulk alone was impressive, but the speed at which it was carried was a constant source of amazement, repeatedly penned in the journal entries. So swift was the pace, one writer registered considerable consternation over his inability to keep sight of his host, while he himself carried only a musket and two umbrellas. No doubt, macho pride and the desire to be quickly finished with a most unpleasant task accounted for much of the speed. However, I am certain – based on my own experience – that the insects further increased the celerity of movement. A voyageur *chanson*, a dialogue between a younger man and his experienced mentor, sheds some light on this. Midway in the lyrical exchange, the older man advises the brash youth, "If the mosquitoes sting your head and deafen your ears with their buzzing, endure them patiently, for they will show you how the Devil will torment you in order to get your poor soul." Endure them they did, for they had little choice. How patiently though? I suspect only as long as it took to rush across those insect-infested trails.

As the demand for North American furs declined, the voyageur departed, leaving behind only a lingering memory of his presence and, of course, the portage trail. Recently, Jim Rowley and I estimated that we had labored over nearly a 1,000 portages each during our thirty years of travel in this canoe country. As a result of our joint venture, we have many shared memories of painful, humorous and inspiring incidents which have occurred on these imposing trails. For me, however, one day's travel always comes to mind with stark, yet satisfying clarity. It occurred in our ninth year of running trips.

Jim and I were taking our group over an unfamiliar chain of lakes. We were travelling on the third day of a seven day trip. We had laid over the previous day on Silence Lake, and everyone was rested and eager to start. Our enthusiasm, however, was soon to be tested.

The lakes we planned to cross appeared nameless on the map. Usually, this spells trouble, yet we were not too concerned. A friend of mine had travelled the same route the previous summer and had reported that the portages, while challenging, were definitely passable. He, however, had not taken fifteen inexperienced canoeists with him.

All morning and well into the afternoon our brief paddles were repeatedly interrupted by lengthy treks across the land. We trudged, slid, stumbled, and bumped our way over one, then another and still another portage: six in all, I believe, although at the time it seemed at least twice that number. The portages were not only covered with fallen trees and heavy plant growth, but making matters worse were trails that appeared to peter out entirely. Six hours later we reached Trant Lake, a serpentine relic from the last glacial moment 10,000 years ago. The portages leading to Trant had gradually eroded our initial enthusiasm and energy. But the worst was yet to come.

Several years earlier, while on a different route Jim and I had crossed the Trant to Kahshahpiwi portage, and we were painfully aware of the deception which lay ahead. The map suggests a relatively easy crossing: a river with two short trails connecting it to the lakes at either end. An unsuspecting canoeist might have justifiably anticipated a rather leisurely crossing. But we knew otherwise and made darn sure that our woeful knowledge was not passed onto the kids. They were, by now, nearly spent, and very irritable as well.

Actually, the passage from Trant to Kahshahpiwi should not have been difficult in late spring when the water is high. But over the years, the wind had pushed large trees into the river forming sylvan barriers that were collecting sizable mounds of a viscous, smelly material through which water indiscernibly seeped. Needless to say, all of this made navigation virtually impossible.

Jim and I were the first to unload. We, too, were tired, but our movement was quick. No, we hadn't gone crazy during this strenuous day; we just wanted to be well ahead of the grumbling which was certain to ensue.

With two packs weighing heavily on my tired frame, I moved out in front of Jim. Jim followed with a pack and canoe.

The portage, nearly a mile, ran between the river on my right and the forest on my left. The trail itself was swampy, difficult to follow, and insect-infested most of the way. I recalled it all too well as I began my trek.

To relieve my suffering while traversing a difficult portage, I developed the practice of visualizing more pleasant moments as I walked. The technique, however, is not entirely perfected and, like the river bed's earthen barriers, is subject to seepage, and I was seeping badly that day.

Trudging along, I pictured the map maker and how he might have derived great humor from the looks of surprise and shock caused by his cartographic omission. And for one fleeting moment, I felt a strong sense of empathy for the cartographer who was denied the droll spectacle that his error was now causing. The feeling, however, quickly waned when it occurred to me that the omission may not have been accidental and that the map-maker responsible from this deliberate rendering derived an occasional chuckle from the thought of some poor soul's unexpected travail. With equal quickness I suspended further speculation on this possibility – moments of adversity do make for grand conspiracies. Besides, my speculation was doing nothing to ease this burden.

The first to cross, I dumped my load and headed back over the trail to issue words of encouragement to our dejected group. Meeting Jim, who was carrying the canoe and puffing hard as he crossed remnants of an abandon beaver dam bridging the river, I extended to him a token offer of assistance. I was exhausted and had no real desire to lug someone else's load.

"I'm okay, but you better check on the others," Jim replied.

"Right," I said, thankful for the reprieve, and thought to myself, "Only fifteen more to go."

At about midpoint on the portage, I met the first member of our group. Mike Herrnstein, a strapping seventeen-year-old, was hobbling toward me minus a boot. Mike had stepped into one of the many bogs on the trail and the suction force which was created when he attempted to remove his foot stripped the boot from his foot. Evidently, he had decided to complete the portage before returning to retrieve his footwear. Judging from the grimace on his face,

Mike's Spartan approach to this problem was causing him considerable discomfort. As I passed, Mike dropped his packs and returned with me to find his boot. As Mike and I searched for the missing gear, his canoe partner emerged from a portion of the trail which weaved into the forest. With a canoe pressing heavily on his aching shoulders, Mike's partner yelled, "How far to go?"

In sheer exasperation, Mike shouted back, "You see where my stuff is? Well, I'm twice as far as you and Mr. Rowley is twice as far as me. And he's still walkin'!"

I may have detected a resigned "Oh" from afar, but perhaps it was simply a beleaguered grunt. Trying days have a way of exacting such sounds of resigned torment.

We finally found the boot, and before resuming our return trip, I gave Mike a reassuring pat on the back. I doubt that it did much good, though. At this point, nothing short of a propitious dispatch to Nirvana could have lifted the young man's nearly broken spirit.

Soon the entire group came into view, one after another having staggered and stumbled out of the forest. I approached cautiously. I feared that someone would sag to the ground in utter despair, pressing me into a reluctant act of gallantry. But, thankfully, none did.

As I travelled down the line, I discharged inspiriting salvos of encouragement to our embattled group. You know, "good job guys, keep it up, your almost there" and the like. My repertoire received mixed reviews. Looks flinging daggers and begging for relief were simultaneously cast my way. So, not wishing to incur the wrath of a caustic tongue,

I quickened my pace, parceling out my trite countenances as I went.

Somehow we all made it. Still, the day's work was not yet done. We had to cross Kahsahpiwi – not any easy task since the crossing was being made increasingly difficult by a stiffing wind and a choppy lake. The paddle across the lake was a struggle, yet we prevailed and set camp on a granite shelf bordered by sentinel-like cliffs. Pure relief showed on the faces of our tired charges as they pitched their tents and prepared for the evening meal.

It had been what Jim and I call "The Day." Invariably, on each of our trips, one day stands out above the others for its difficulty. On that day the emotional adhesive, which normally serves one quite well in the face of adversity, is pried at so relentlessly that it is all one can do to resist the urge to quit. But a day like this also presents an opportunity for our young canoeists to see a part of themselves which is rarely ever revealed.

After dinner, I walked around our camp surveying the mood of the group. The usual mirthfulness evident on other evenings was much subdued. Everyone was tired, and deservedly so. Nevertheless, each member of our group seemed to be quietly assessing the significance of their accomplishment that day.

I climbed to a ridge overlooking the camp. It was a peaceful evening. The loons had started their playful serenade, and the wind provided an accompaniment as it worked its way gently through the stately stand of spruce and fir which surrounded me. I sat there for about a half-hour when

I heard someone approaching off to my left. Turning, I saw a young lady named Teresa trying, quite unsuccessfully, to approach unnoticed.

"Mind if I come over?" Teresa asked when she saw me watching her.

"No, come ahead," I replied. "How ya doing?"

"Great! Tired, but great."

"Pretty rough day, huh?" I commented, figuring that I would let her establish the direction of the conversation.

"Yeah, but it was worth it," Teresa said. "I'm really glad I came back this year."

Teresa had been with us the previous year, and in the nine years we had run trips she had been our only casualty – a broken leg. Undaunted, however, by that painful experience, she had been one of the first to sign up for this year's trip.

"How's that?" I asked.

"Just look around you. Isn't that reason enough?" She answered, but in a way that made me think that there was more to come. And I waited.

"It sure is beautiful here, but that's not the real reason," Teresa admitted. "Last year when I broke my leg, I felt like a real fool…when it wasn't hurting, that is. Besides, it happened on a day like today, a hard day. And there I was hobbling and being carried across all those portages." Pausing slightly, she added, "Yeah, a real fool."

"Hey, think about me. Those were some of the most difficult portages I've ever done. You're not exactly the easy cargo to tote," I said, half in jest and half deadly serious.

And we both laughed.

"I imagine," she agreed. "Anyway, I was kinda scared to try again. But when my cousin agreed to go on this year's trip with me, I just couldn't back out."

Not wanting to break Teresa's train of thought, I remained silent. She continued for awhile before getting to the point she was trying to make all along.

"Today was special for me, you know," she said, beaming with pride. "I found out something important about myself. Making all those portages showed me…no, I mean I showed myself that I could do a lot more than I ever thought possible."

We looked at each other for a moment and she knew that I understand.

"Well, fine and dandy. She did it, but what about me?" you say. "How would I fare on one of those imposing trails?"

Imagine for a moment: Let me take you across your first portage ever. Admittedly, it will be a difficult one, although not the worst of the lot.

You begin by slipping your canoe close to a shoreline covered with large granite rocks. Since jagged rocks extend submerged in the lake along the shore, you depart your craft knee-deep in water. The precaution is necessary to avoid damaging the bottom of the canoe.

The canoe is then pulled closer to the shore, yet you still stand in several inches of water as your partner loads you with gear. First the straps of a forty pound, soft pack are pulled over your shoulders, and with the pack pressing against your straining back, you begin to sense a bit of the discomfort you will endure for the next twenty minutes. But there is more to come. A second pack – weighing considerably more than the first since it contains food and metal utensils – is hung on your front. The straps of the two packs now crisscross your shoulders, cutting equally in opposite directions. Then come the incidentals. Three damp life jackets are strung over your head and rest loosely around your neck. And with a paddle clasped in each hand, you carefully make your way to the shore over slippery algae covered rocks.

Your little stroll through the dense forest begins with a thirty degree climb covering about forty yards. Slowly, you move from one granite step to another. I use this term loosely: they are not steps at all, but an assortment of protrusions in the earth's crust. Their shapes vary greatly. Some are round and smooth, while others are jagged and sharp as a chisel's edge. Too few are flat and level, a welcome relief to an unsure foot. And all are covered with moss and lichen. If you are fortunate, it has not rained recently, for moisture makes the covered granite slippery and the climb twice as treacherous.

Reaching the top, you see a winding flat – an easy walk by comparison. At first, your pace slows, since you are now trying to catch your breath from the initial climb. The hesitation, however, is brief: an army of mosquitoes, black flies and no-see-ums is attacking the exposed portions of your skin. If you are smart, and many aren't, before starting your *journey, you had put on your sweat shirt and drawn the hood tightly around your head. But alas, the little thieves still find places to rob you of your precious blood, to say nothing of the itching welts they leave behind. Still, you have the better part of the ordeal. Your partner must contend with all of this and the canoe, too. The amplified buzz of mosquitoes inside the upturned canoe ranks as one of life's major nuisances.*

About now you curse the person who talked you into this masochistic venture, in the first place. Your anger, however, is closely followed by silent pleas for mercy. But no one is there to help you except yourself. Quickly, you chide yourself for indulging in such a pathetic display of self-pity, and somehow your tired legs continue to carry your tethered body down the switching trail.

Just when it seems that you have mastered this grueling test, the swamp appears. And down you travel to what you are convinced is the denizen of the damned.

Fallen trees have been placed across the swamp's wet surface in a poor attempt to construct a crude bridge. But they are covered with slime where even the most sure-footed mountain goat would have great difficulty crossing without slipping off. So you trudge on finding footing where you can, but mostly with the sheer force of will, you wallow through, knee-deep in muck.

The physical demand is one thing; the swamp's smell is something else. The fetid odor of decay cracks your nose, drawing a feeling of nausea from your tightened stomach. You gag, but manage to hold down any putrid liquid; this is neither the time nor the place for a mawkish affliction.

By the time you reach the other side, sweat is pouring from your body. It is much too warm for your sweat shirt, but the alternative is even worse. As you climb from the swamp, the packs' straps have started to chafe your shoulders. You are tempted to drop the front pack, but you reject this idea when you think of the difficulty involved in returning to retrieve it. And you plod on.

Reaching the top of the rise, you proceed down the trail. Your eyes are focused upward. You are anxiously looking for something: that resplendent crack of blue between the trees signaling journey's end. And there it is. Your heart beats faster, your steps quicken and your body gains an unexpected surge of strength. At the water's edge you dump your load and bend over with your hands on your knees. You have just trudged, slid and pushed your way over three-eights of a mile portage.

Close behind, your partner rambles down the trail and into the lake, where he flips the canoe into the water. Although the trip has taken its toll on your strength, both you and your mate move rapidly loading the canoe. The insects are rallying for another assault, a confrontation you would sooner avoid. With your partner in the bow, you push the canoe out onto the lake, hopping in as you give it a final thrust.

And out you drift onto a lake more beautiful than the last.

Over the years, I have seen the marrow of life revealed on these portages: rage, despair and tears; sweat and sweat on sweat; and pain pleading for merciful surrender spurned only by an indomitable will to carry on. And at the end, I have sensed that quiet pride one gains from knowing that limits, once thought insurmountable, have been exceeded by relying solely upon one's own fortitude.

A few years ago, I took a trip with Jim and two friends, George Dirner and Chris Douglas. From the beginning of our trip, it was abnormally hot – the temperatures ranging in the nineties – and the cloudless skies made that days seem like we were on a trek through the desert, rather than in the midst of a lush oasis. By late afternoon on the fourth day, our strength was nearly sapped and we were running almost entirely on giddy energy. One portage remained before setting camp, and it would end up being the most taxing of the trip.

Jim and I arrived at the portage first. As I loaded him with gear, the second canoe pulled alongside. Carrying two packs and gear, Jim headed out. I lifted our canoe to my shoulders and turned to my left, hitting George squarely on the head. He sank to the ground, dazed. Chris, who was on his maiden canoe trip and by then quite overwhelmed by the whole experience, looked on in utter disbelief.

"My God, this is a nightmare!" he bellowed.

And you know he was right. That is exactly what some days are like in this majestic wilderness.

THE END

My Solo

I sit facing the west on a granite shelf on the largest island on Robinson Lake, the twelfth day on my solo canoe trip in Canada's Quetico Provincial Park. It is an early September evening. Tomorrow I will leave these quiet waters and enter a part of the Park where motors are still legal. I watch and listen. My senses are unified into the single purpose of fully living this solitary experience.

Moments earlier the sun dropped behind the tree lined, serrated boundary between water and sky. I watch as a dusty yellow sky perches itself on this coniferous nest. Off to the south, Venus rises early on her quick autumn journey, and at her last issues a flirtatious wink before retiring behind the now darkened horizon.

The moon, almost full, ventures forth from the southeast. As it reaches the peak of its climb, it claims itself as the evening's main attraction.

A whisper of wind from the northeast gently caresses my cheek and, moving over the lake, forms subtle ripples that create light and dark patterns from the moon's brilliant light.

Forest sounds pause from across the lake as if to observe a moment of reverent silence, and then briefly continue their playful serenade. A single loon issues a final call, a lonely sound, as if harbingering winter's deceptively rapid advance.

The night sky seems to expand as, one by one, stars push their way through the blanket of darkness, until a tapestry of heavenly-inspired bodies float overhead. These lights of night, barely noticed in today's urban world, offer a worthy encore to the magnificent performance that had just unfolded. Suddenly, I am overcome with an irrefutable awareness of my smallness.

I sit in complete awe of this celestial spectacle and my soul is at peace.

My fifteen day journey began on Moose Lake in the BWCAW. Departing early on the last day of August, my step-son, Mark, who was vacationing in the area with his father, motored me to the Canadian entry point at Prairie Portage. There I paid my entry duties and purchased a fishing license. And soon, I was off, paddling and portaging my canoe and gear across Bailey Bay. It was a beautiful day, sunny and nearly windless. I crossed the large sandy portage leading to Burke Lake, paddled north up Burke, and portaged twice out onto North Bay of Basswood Lake. There I set my first camp.

The region in which I was travelling is referred to as Quetico-Superior. Quetico-Superior lies in the northeastern corner of Minnesota and northwestern Ontario. The United States' portion of the area is called the Boundary Waters Canoe Area Wilderness, while its Canadian counterpart is Quetico Provincial Park. Together this wilderness encompasses two million acres with nearly 2,000 interconnected lakes. This area is the largest of its kind in North America, making it perfectly suited for wilderness canoe travel.

While the first day of my solo experience had begun on a calm, sunny day and was most uneventful, the second day proved to be quite the opposite. I rose and left early. I could tell that the weather was changing and I wanted to advance as far as I could before a storm thwarted my progress. As expected, lightning forced me to set an early camp on Sunday Lake.

After setting camp, I read and napped for the better part of the afternoon. When I rose to begin preparing for dinner, I discovered that a large, black bear had rifled through one of my packs and was now sitting in the middle of my campsite. Initially startled, I quickly devised a plan to handle this unexpected situation. My plan, unfortunately, proved highly ineffective. Although the plan initially seemed well conceived, its execution left something to be desired. It was apparent that the bear had no intention to go anywhere. Furthermore, he was showing signs of aggression. At one point it appeared that my future was limited to the present, and I prepared myself for a premature end to what then seemed like an ill-conceived venture to start with.

But no attack came. I steadied myself and regained my composure. I looked that old bear squarely in the eye, probably not the smartest of moves, and dropped my tent and packed my gear. As my movement quickened, I offered my intruder an improvised oration designed to both cajole and distract.

Throughout my rather disjointed oration, the bear just stood there studiously watching me as I babbled on. Finally, with everything ready for what I hoped to be a quick and uneventful departure, I turned my canoe, pushed it into the water, loaded my gear and paddled out on to the lake About fifty yards from the shore, I looked back. My nemesis had wandered down to the water and was lounging lazily on the sandy beach. I felt fortunate to have this encounter end so well.

I paddled down the lake to the next portage. Two couples were camped there almost directly on the trail. As I unloaded my gear preparing to cross, I shouted a warning to the camp's occupants.

"You might want to think about hanging your food packs high tonight," I advised. "There's a bear down the lake, and he is likely heading in this direction."

Sometimes a look tells an entire story, and this was one of those moments. Two women were in this group, wives I presumed. Judging from the look on their faces, a wilderness canoe trip had not been their first choice for a summer's vacation, and now with an unwanted visitor fast approaching their lack of enthusiasm was quickly turning to dread. As I headed across the portage, I speculated about the conversations that likely ensued that night in those two tents. It occurred to me that the tone alone may have unknowingly worked to their advantage, encouraging that old bear to wander on as he approached their camp.

I portaged and paddled to Silence Lake, getting there as the sun dropped behind the silhouetted horizon. I selected a favorite island camp that I hoped might provide me some protection from another unwanted intruder. Although feeling a little disoriented, I still managed to set a good camp. My appetite was gone; after starting a fire, I satisfied myself with a cup of coffee for dinner. My mind was racing. Central to my cogitating was a reoccurring recrimination that questioned this whole solo-business in the first place. With nothing resolved, I headed to bed, hoping for a deep and undisturbed sleep.

By morning, I was still feeling out of sorts. I had planned my trip with a safety value. I had mapped out three possible routes, each a longer extension of the last. The weather and my ability to handle the canoe alone would ultimately determine the route taken. Since the previous day's unnerving event was causing me serious consternation about my trip, my plan's flexibility permitted me to stay put on day three. It was a good decision and one that allowed me to collect my wits and renew my resolve.

It was a beautiful late summer's day. That afternoon a party of two canoes passed close to my island camp. We shared a greeting. They would be that last people I would see for the next three days.

On the morning of the fourth day, I paddled from Silence, the northern most lake on the S-chain, out onto Agnes Lake, one of the longest lakes in the Quetico. My initial encounter with Agnes had occurred on my first trip to this wilderness. My good friend Jim Rowley and I organized our first canoe trip for high school students, a venture that would span the next twenty-five years.

On that initial trip, Agnes taught us an important lesson that we would never forget. Looking out onto the lake from the narrows between Silence and Agnes, we could see white on the water's surface, but it didn't seem that bad. We headed out onto the lake, but quickly discover that we were wrong. What could have ended disastrously was avoided by a quick, corrective decision and a little bit of old-fashioned good luck. We got our party safely to shore, and all afternoon watched Agnes display what seemed to us a protest to our very presence. We never made this mistake again, always mindful of nature's controlling interest in this pristine wilderness.

I thought about that encounter as I paddled north up Agnes Lake. Fortunately, I was blessed with a day with no wind, and, thus, a peaceful paddle lasting half of the day. Moving off the big water, I headed my canoe north on the west channel of the Agnes River. The river and its four portages emptied into Murdock Lake, a perfect setting for my third camp. Again, I decided on an island, one that we had named Lemon on an earlier trip for reasons I can no longer recall.

Murdock had provided the most humorous memory of all our high school ventures. On the second year running trips, a young man named Scott Popoff hooked a Northern Pike while casually casting from the shoreline across from our camp. He and his canoe mate had managed to get the twenty pound fish next to the shore when his fishing line broke. Scott promptly jumped into the lake and grabbed the fish. As Jim and I approached in our canoe, he was staggering out of the water, his arms tightly hugging his massive catch.

(Given a Pike's needle-like teeth, another disaster was luckily dodged.)

As we departed our canoe, the two freshmen boys were vigorously delivering alternating blows with their wooden paddles to the head of this impressive fish. Jim walked up to where the boys were gesticulating and said, "Nice fish, but given its size probably not a particularly good eater." The boys paused, appearing to reflect on their hasty decision. Scott looked at Jim sheepishly and asked, "Do you think we can revive it, Mr. Rowley?" Jim just chuckled.

That night, not wishing to waste nature's bounty, we cooked and ate our second meal of the evening. The fish fed the entire group, with some to spare. For Scott, this was the first fresh-water fish he had ever caught.

I decided to layover on Murdock. That evening I decided to set up my fishing pole and troll above the channel emptying out of the lake. The Bass that I caught was a much appreciated addition to the evening meal. The food provisions that I had packed for this trip were very basic and were lacking in protein.

On day six, I headed north. As I paddled the narrows that lead to Kawnippi Lake, I glanced to my left and spotted a large racked moose emerge from the woods and wade into the water. Suddenly, he was totally submerged save for his head and that large rack. He swam swiftly for the opposite shore of the narrows. I turned my canoe and paddled powerfully on a line intended to intersect his path. I wanted to get a good photograph of this animal, but he was too fast for me. I could only watch as he emerged from the water and trotted into the woods quickly concealing himself in the dense forest vegetation.

At the time, I wondered why it was so important for me to take this photograph. With greater ease, I could have gone to a zoo and with little effort taken a perfectly good picture of this "wild" animal.

There is, however, something deeply satisfying about spotting an animal in the wild. Whether it is the effort required to make this sighting or solely the animal itself, one is rewarded by seeing a display of strength and independence devoid of any self-awareness. In our Disney-saturated world, it is tempting to ascribe human traits to animals when describing them in their natural setting. I suspect, when doing so we are also subconsciously identifying characteristics that we would like to claim for our better selves. At any rate, the stance of an animal in the wild and the high hang of its head are distinctly different from any of its kind I have seen elsewhere. I guess this is why that picture seemed so important to me. But I have it still here in my memory, as distinct in detail as if captured yesterday.

I paddled north on Kawnippi. This water was new to me, and I was now committing myself to the middle-route option of my trip. Kawnippi was a long push to the next portage, so I decided to drag a fishing line. As I paddled, a walleye struck it and in short order I had secured my evening meal.

As I approached the short portage that would turn me south, I saw two canoeists crossing in my direction. I paused for a moment about fifty yards from the portage. Sitting in my canoe, gently bobbing from side to side, I felt an acute sense of violation. These people were the first I had encountered in three days. This was my experience, my wilderness, and what right had they to intrude on the solitude I was now enjoying. The feeling was fleeting and by the time we crossed paths we shared a cordial exchange before moving along on our respective routes.

As I carried my gear, I smiled while savoring the thought of the three days of solitude which I had been allotted. It was the longest I had ever experienced. Remembering those three days later, I fully appreciated Thoreau's comment: "I never found the companion that was so companionable as solitude."

I set camp that evening on Cairn Lake, the first of three long lakes leading to the next day's destination, Kahshahpiwi Lake. That evening the air lay heavy with humidity and a small breeze crept across the lake. Crouching on an island point by the water cleaning the utensils used to prepare my excellent walleye meal, I studied the changing light along the horizon. And, suddenly, all movement in the universe seemed to stop. I tilted my head trying to catch the slightest sound in the air. Total stillness with its accompanying silence had captured the moment.

I thought to myself, "Could I shout? Could I break the spell?" But nothing came. It appeared to me that nature was in complete control and nothing that I could do would pierce this impenetrable, still silence.

I broke camp early, travelling over Stark and Keefer Lakes before arriving in the early afternoon at my destination on Kahshahpiwi Lake.

I set camp on a flat, granite shelf with easy access to the water. That evening lying in my sleeping bag, I began hearing the oddest noise: a galloping sound outside my tent. Even today, I have no idea what the source of this sound was, but I remember lying there as I pictured miniature horses circling the tent.

I had originally intended to move due south, completing my trip on familiar lakes. However, the previous evening I began studying my map. The map showed a westerly route leading to McIntyre Lake, one of the most picturesque lakes in the Park. The route was new to me, but following my layover day on Kahshahpiwi, I was feeling well rested, more confident, and adventuresome. On the ninth day of my trip, I decided to modify my original plan and head toward Joyce Lake, the first of several lakes leading to McIntyre. By committing to the Joyce-Marj-Burt chain, my travel-hand, as they say in poker, was all in. I had committed to the longest route. And it would become a day that my feet would remember for quite some time.

The portage off Kahshahpiwi leading to a small unnamed lake in this demanding chain was neither easy to locate, nor to traverse. Kahshahpiwi was sharply carved by the last ice age, and as a result was made up of quickly climbing walls on both sides of the lake. Once I found the portage and made the steep climb, things didn't improve much over the course of the day. This was the day of my trip where the word portage showed its full meaning.

The portage is the land trail that links the network of lakes in this wilderness. Since my equipment consisted of a canoe, three soft packs, two paddles and life jackets, I had been forced to double portage. In short, this means that I had to walk each portage three times: twice with gear and the canoe, and once to acquire that gear which I left behind on the first trip.

The portages connecting this chain of lakes proved to be long and varied in their degree of difficulty. Later, I calculated that I walked six miles that day. Now this may not seem like much to an experienced backpacker or even a casual hiker, but this is not your normal wilderness stroll.

As I started on the second of seven portages, I chuckled softly, remembering the expressions of disbelief on faces of our young, first-time canoeists as they traveled across their initial portage, one that was not particularly difficult. The moment of humor quickly passed. I had begun this portage with a slight climb over an assortment of granite protrusions from the earth's crust. The shapes varied, but none allowed for stable footing. Adding to my difficulty was that most of the granite surfaces were covered with moss and lichen, and the morning dampness made them slippery.

Once I reached the top of the rise, I was on my way down again, this time to a swamp that spanned about one hundred yards. Previous canoeists had tried to make the crossing more manageable. Downed trees had been dragged lengthwise over the swampy area in an attempt to construct a crude bridge. That effort, though admirable, proved quite inadequate. The bridge's surface was wet and the slightest miscalculation could have easily put me into muck up to my knees. With a pack on my back and a canoe on my shoulders, I would likely find myself barely able to move. Fortunately, I avoided this worst case situation.

The fetid smell of decay, however, was unavoidable. To combat this unpleasantness, I conjured thoughts of sweeter fragrances as I trundled over the makeshift bridge.

Traveling this country in September allowed me one advantage. If I had been in this swamp in the spring or early summer, I would have had to contend with an army of biting insects

I reached the end of the swamp and headed down the trail. The trail was flat and dry, but turned sharply in several places. This was particularly perplexing on the portage crossing that involved carrying the canoe. More than once, the turn was so tight that my canoe got lodged between two trees. Awkwardly, I had to back up with no visibility as to where I was stepping.

As this sinuous part of the trail ended, I found myself descending again into a swampy area, which fortunately was shorter and much less taxing.

Up again I went over a short rise and then I saw the crack of blue between the trees that signaled journey's end. Down to the lake I traveled, wading into the water before flipping the canoe off my shoulders. If I had been with a group of our young canoeists, I would have been finished. But since I was alone, back I headed across the portage, twice repeating the first crossing.

This portage was the worst part of my day, but not by much. Each of the remaining trails had unique aspects of difficulty, characteristics that would never improve in the coming years. As demanding as the day had been, this route allowed me to visit McIntyre, and at the end of the day, as I camped on a large island with its magnificent view of the lake, the effort seemed worthwhile.

On my second night on the island, I decided to sleep out under the open sky. The sky was clear and the stars shown brightly. I drifted asleep tracking the movement of a satellite working its way across the night sky. By morning, a dense fog had set in.

At this point on my trip, I had traveled over two new sets of lakes. Sitting on McIntyre, while studying my map the previous night, I realized that I had an opportunity to explore a third new area before heading in. On past trips, when camped on this island site, we always paddled to the southern end of McIntyre, taking the portages into Robinson Lake. Then we travelled north on Robinson to reach a favorite island camp.

My map showed a short cut through a westerly bay off the main body of the lake, leading to a river that emptied into the north end of Robinson. On the map short portages were marked at each end of the river. More importantly, the river was named, a good indication that the passage was regularly used.

As I began my portage into the McIntyre River, I expected a short paddle before portaging again at the other end. Before starting, my biggest concern had been the portages. I quickly discovered that the river was actually the greater challenge. Every assortment of wilderness biomass had made its way into the river bed, forcing me to exit my canoe into the river chest deep water. As I dragged and lifted my canoe over repeated obstacles, I recalled Humphrey Bogart in *African Queen*. And I hoped that I would not discover, upon my ascent from the water, the same spectacle that had caused him such alarm. Thankfully, I did not.

This route into Robinson shortened my travel day significantly. Despite the river's natural impediments, I continued to use the river in the years ahead.

Day thirteen marked the beginning of my return to civilization. As I began my paddle south to the Tuck and Basswood rivers, I felt conflicted about the end of my trip. I found that I enjoyed travelling alone. Certainly, both the physical challenge and sense of adventure had been important. But more than that, discovering the comfort I felt with my own company was especially satisfying.

Admittedly, by then, I was savoring the thought of a cold beer and a large steak, definitely two of civilization's better offerings. But if I had had provisions for a few more days, I believe that I could have forgone those Ely delights a little longer.

As I paddled into the Turk River, I sensed a big change in the weather would occur soon. By the time I reached the Basswood River the wind had stiffened from the East, and I found myself paddling directly into it. Usually, when encountering a windy day, a canoeist is glad to be off a large lake and traveling on a more protected river. Given the direction of the wind and its increasing intensity, the Basswood River provided little relief.

My target for the day was an island camp on Basswood Lake just off Horse Portage, a long portage that bypassed several imposing rapids at the head of the Basswood River. So I pushed on into the wind, portaging around Lower Basswood Falls and over Wheelbarrow Portage. As I reached a bend in the river that turned me facing due east, my progress was halted. I could see the beginning of Horse Portage, but it might as well have been in California. I wasn't going to get there on this day.

I hunkered down at a point on leeward side of a natural granite wall. After assembling a crude camp in this crowded space, I spent the rest of the day and evening drinking coffee and jotting thoughts in my notebook.

The next morning, the wind had subsided enough to allow me to paddle the 200 hundred yards or so to Horse Portage. This portage is wide and offers fairly good footing. Its difficulty comes from its length, over a mile. Over the years I took Horse Portage a number of times with high school groups that I guided. My partner and I disliked lugging our gear over this long portage, so we decided to borrow a page from Tom Sawyer, determining that this portage provided an excellent fence substitute for a metaphorical white washing. To facilitate our plan we created the Miler's Club. To become a member of this august group, a canoeist had to carry nonstop two packs and a canoe over this long crossing. The successful group members received a T-shirt transfer signifying their membership in the Club. The kids seemed to relish the challenge, and we frequently had more eager participants than we had canoes to accommodate them. And, of course, Jim and I enjoyed walking that trail with only a single pack.

Although having to double portage made this a three and a half-mile crossing, I appreciated the activity. Completing my first crossing, I encountered four canoeists who were camped just off the trail. After completing my final crossing, we engaged in a conversation. The group's leader first read about the Quetico in an outdoors magazine. He had been eagerly anticipating this initial trip for several years, but unfortunately the bad weather had limited his group's travel. Although they were amply packed by a local outfitter, their culinary options had been limited by the intermittent rain. They had struggled to start a fire and had to resort to eating items that did not require cooking. I started a fire for them. By this point they had accumulated three days of meals and proceeded to prepare all of them. I was invited to join them. I was grateful since my provisions were nearly gone.

The start of Horse Portage faced the western arm of Basswood Lake, one of the largest lakes in this wilderness. The wind had again intensified, and by late afternoon was pushing ocean sized waves toward the shore. I stood helplessly watching this aquatic tumult, when from behind me I heard the approach of a second party. I turned around and saw four bearded men purposefully trudging down the trail to water. These boys looked like they belonged in this wilderness. One of them nodded in my direction, then addressing his companion said, "I sure had a hankering for a steak at Elna's tonight." The others grunted an agreement. Promptly, one of the boys pulled out what appeared to be a couple of marijuana joints, lighting and passing them around. After scanning the lake a second time, they climbed into their canoes and headed out into this setting fit for a leviathan. I have to say, I was duly impressed by both their resolve and decisiveness. But I also wondered if I was witnessing a last hurrah foolishly executed.

That evening I constructed a voyageur style shelter with my canoe and tarp. As I lay in my sleeping bag underneath my canoe, I listened to the wind's tormenting whine. Eternity captured my thoughts as I drifted off to sleep.

Around five in the morning, something woke me. The wind had stopped, and the sudden sound of silence had jolted me awake. I turned my canoe and pushed it into the water, repacked my sleeping bag, and loaded my packs. Hoping for a change in the weather, I had left everything ready for a quick departure the previous night.

The sky was an early morning grey, and the lake's surface was mirror smooth. Nature's changing face never ceased to amaze me.

I headed for Pipestone Bay, taking, at the end of the bay, two portages into Fall Lake, where I had left my van. During my last hour, the wind had begun to increase, forcing me to hold my two paddles together with both of my hands and paddle kayak-style across the lake.

This was the fifteenth day, of one of my life's most memorable moments.

Before recently revising this essay, which had been first written forty years ago, I reviewed the notebook I kept on my trip. From the pages composed on the day I was forced to stop on the Basswood River, I wrote, "As good as this experience is, it will, with time, likely become more than it is now." Reflection always seems to add a broadening perspective, particularly when an experience touches one's emotional core.

I was a high school history teacher. As my wilderness experiences continued and expanded into other settings, I became increasingly aware of how we frequently gave short shrift to the frontiersmen who inhabited this land when it was only wilderness. This neglect seemed a disservice to a more thorough understanding of our national experience. If nothing else, we would have gained a better awareness of the part of that character that rejected security and safety, embracing instead physical challenge and its accompanying danger.

Of course, times change, and with it what we hold important. Today a sentimental orgasm or a digital distraction seems a sufficient substitute for the self-reliance required in this earlier period.

But perhaps the yearning for the self-reliance so central to this man of the open sky resides in all of us, just waiting for an opportunity to spring forth and take charge of the situation at hand. A wilderness trip like mine provides a person with a fleetingly taste of the unfettered freedom, simplicity, and, yes, risks that earlier man's lives embraced. I think this is justification enough for the preservation of undeveloped areas like the Quetico-Superior wilderness. If we decide to play fast and loose with the integrity of wild places, we risk not only destroying the stage, but with it, the opportunity for each of us to better appreciate those qualities which were so central to our national's story.

Many arguments have been offered extolling the value of wild places. For the transcendentalist Thoreau, the woods was a place to learn deliberate living; for history Frederick Jackson Turner, the frontier was a safety valve for potential social upheaval, and the basis for America's national character and strength; for conservationist Aldo Leopold, the land was an instructive lesson on ethics unto itself.

As compelling as each of these arguments is, I best like one told to me by a man that I spoke with briefly after our first crossing of what we came to call Big Agony portage into Sunday Lake. He likely had quickly assessed our rookie status. Our Levis and Converse tennis shoes were probably the dead give away.

With a distinct northern Minnesota accent, he said, "Boys, there is one thing about these lakes that you don't find in what folks call civilization. You always know exactly why you feel good and why you feel bad. You don't need a psychologist or complicated theory to help you figure that out." Then pausing for a moment, I suspect for emphasis, he concluded, "Yes, I guess, that more than anything else is the true gift of this wilderness."

He winked and chuckled, and headed out over Big Agony in the opposite direction.

After thirty years of travel in this canoe country wilderness, I would only add to that, "Amen!"

THE END

Writer's note: Regarding the essay My Solo, my trip encompassed 85 miles over 30 lakes, 5 rivers and 45 portages. It included 9 travel days and 6 layover days. For any one contemplating such a trip, it was a perfect balance between of difficulty and repose.

The Bear

The incident involving the bear described in My Solo was profoundly meaningful. For a moment I thought that I might die. The reader will find below an elaboration of this encounter.

He looked at me and I looked back at him. His triangular snout twitched slightly, apparently sensing a smell that he found disagreeable. But his black, dopey face showed no sign of agitation or alarm. Then again, why should it? He outweighed me by at least 100 pounds, and his physical prowess was unquestionably superior to mine. If I could have exited unnoticed, I would have. But the intruder was eating my food, and I wasn't about to fast for the next thirteen days of this, my first solo canoe trip. I had to do something – AND QUICKLY.

I am a high school history teacher. And as a result, on numerous occasions I have quoted Franklin Roosevelt's famous line about fear being all one really had to fear. But I'll bet you FDR never encountered a situation the likes of this while wandering around the wilds of his Campobello retreat. If he had, he may have added to his memorable encouragement, "and big, black bears foraging through your food pack for a final repast before their long winter's nap."

This most unsettling situation occurred smack dab in the middle of one of the most peaceful and pristine wildernesses I have ever traveled – Canada's Quetico Provincial

Park. For the past eight years, I had traveled the lakes on both the American and Canadian side of this adjoining canoe country wilderness, mostly as a guide for teenage trips that my friend Jim Rowley and I organized.

I suppose it was five years earlier when I first entertained the notion of soloing these lakes. Although I had toyed with the idea since, the time never seemed right. There was always something else to do or someplace else to go, underlined, no doubt, by my lack of gumption to try.

Then, last year, I took a leave-of-absence from teaching. During the final week of a typically hot and humid Ohio August, I was struck with, what seemed at the time, a brilliant idea. It occurred to me that by late summer most everyone had had their fill of wilderness adventure. It was perfect. If I left immediately, I could capture the final weeks of good weather and have the place to myself to boot. It was a deal I couldn't resist.

Filled with child-like enthusiasm, I readied my gear, pitched my canoe atop my van and headed north.

I started my trip on the last day of August. Several canoe parties were returning to civilization as I embarked. As I crossed Prairie Portage, a canoeist crossing in the opposite direction asked, "How long are you out for?"

And I responded, "Fifteen days.

"Boy, it must be great,"

To whit, I said confidently, "It's going to be."

But little did I know what was in store. If I had, I might have modified somewhat my optimistic prediction.

It was a perfect day to begin my adventure. Although the calendar still acknowledged summer's reign, hints of autumn were clearly evident in this North Country wilderness. Amongst the dominant spruce and fir, scattered patches of birch and aspen had begun to turn yellow, and the air even had traces of autumn's heavy, moist fragrance. While I paddled my canoe across Bailey Bay from the Canadian entry point at Prairie Portage, the sun shined brightly, occasionally veiled by slow drifting cotton ball clouds and a slight breeze tickled my back. I was grateful for this tranquil reception, since I was not exuding with confidence about handling my canoe alone on open water.

I have to admit; I really enjoyed the looks of envy I got from the canoeists heading in. And I suppose I felt a little cocky, too—a voyageur reincarnated and all that. But by the time I got to the first portage, my enraptured audience had dwindled to nothing, and I was left on this airy stage asking myself why I had embarked on this venture in the first place. I knew that I wasn't indulging in a masochistic test of my endurance. I had done that when I was younger, and I had discovered that it hurt. And I wasn't traveling alone simply as a macho expression of self-reliance. But what then was the main reason? All my speculations kept hitting a dead end, so I abandoned my inquiry and pushed on.

Heading north, I paddled up Burke Lake, portaged again and set an early camp on North Bay of Basswood Lake. After pitching my tent and arranging my packs, I spent the rest of the afternoon perched on granite shelf sharpening my senses to the wilderness's subtle sounds and movements and jotting down in my notebook every sagely thought I could force from my mind.

After an hour, with mind oozing only syrupy sentiments, I concluded that my enterprise was suffering from what economists call diminishing returns, so I turned to more mundane matters and busied myself with camp chores. Retrieving water from the lake, firewood from the forest, and a box of Kraft macaroni and cheese from my pack, I prepared the first of many simple meals which would follow in the days ahead. And for entertainment I watched a raft of loons display and call in the bay just off my island camp.

Retiring early, I lay in my sleeping bag, shifting from side to side. When I eventually found my body's proper fit to the earth, I contemplated the grand adventure awaiting me. My anxious thoughts drifted into surreal images, finally fading into the deep darkness of sleep.

While my first day had been calm and uneventful, the second was to be quite the opposite. I woke to a leaden sky and a fine drizzle. Forgoing breakfast, I packed hurriedly and moved from my island camp, paddling and portaging over the first three in a chain of lakes leading to my planned destination, Silence Lake.

Suddenly from the southwest, a rush of wind and breaks of lightening stopped my progress, forcing me to take refuge in the forest along the shore. For the better part of an hour, the thunderous claps continued, echoing robustly at the end of the lake.

While the shoreline cover provided little protection from the rain, as inadequate as my shelter was, I was glad to be on the shore and not the water-bound target of some errant bolt of lightening. Then, with equal quickness the storm subsided, and the sun's warmth caressed my cold, dank skin.

I portaged onto the next lake and decided to set camp. The day was still early, but the combination of the sun's slumberous effect and my compelling urge to loaf got the best of me. Besides, the wind was beginning to force small patches of white on the water's surface, and I wasn't about to take on Nature's challenge, schedule or not.

I selected a rare sandy spot on the shore to beach my canoe. As all camping primers instruct, the tasks came first. I unloaded my gear, overturned my canoe on the shore, pitched my tent, and readied my packs for the evening meal. Then with all chores dutifully discharged, I reclined on the sand while reading and dozing lightly in the afternoon sun.

Judging from the sun's arc, I guessed that it was about five o'clock when I rose and walked to the rear of my tent, where my packs had been temporarily arranged. My eyes were affixed to the ground a few yards ahead of my gait. As I approached the packs, something seemed odd. One stuff sack containing food lay open on the ground. I didn't recall removing it from its canvas pack, but, then again, my memory had been known to fail me at times.

Scratching the side of my beard, I looked up and there he was: a big black, furry bear, no more than ten yards from where I stood—the first I had ever seen in this wilderness. Unfazed by my presence, he just sat there casually forking with one very long claw the contents of one very small package of hot chocolate into his mouth.

Finally acknowledging me, he raised his head and glanced at me as if to say, "Can I help you with anything." His seemingly congeniality was momentarily reassuring, and I regained my composure and thought quickly. I had anticipated such an encounter often before and I had a plan. However, as with most plans that fall far short of their preconceived design, mine was to prove no exception.

I had to establish the dominate position – I remember now thinking at the time how ridiculous this seemed while standing only a few yards from an animal that significantly out weighed me. Yet, I would try. I reached for all my thunder. Even today, I am sure that it started with the terrifying roar of a lion, but by the time it spilled into the air it had been somehow reduced to a whimpering behest – and one that was no less nauseating than, "Please get out of here you pest."

"Did I really do that?" I thought. "Oh my god, I'm in for it now."

But he returned only an annoyed look. And I sighed gratefully, for I had expected much worse for my pathetic display.

Over the years, I have observed that humans have a rather interesting faculty for self-preservation. When confronted squarely with their own ridiculousness, they invariably respond with a face-saving act of aggression. By now, with that old bear ignoring me entirely, as he slobbered over the last remnants of my hot chocolate, I was taken with an indomitable urge to redeem myself. Wiping the simper from my face, I fortified myself for a more forceful approach to the problem.

"By golly," I reasoned, "I am the brains here and no damn bear is going to screw up my trip. No sirree."

It was, I thought, a good start at the self-deception required to handle this sort of unnerving situation. And with human arrogance firmly intact, I pushed forth a very forceful admonishment, sprinkled, of course, with some well placed expletives. I suspect even bears must know that warnings punctuated with colored language are to be taken seriously, for he promptly lumbered down into the woods – about twenty-five yards of it, that is.

Not wishing to press my luck, I hurriedly collected the tattered remains of my hot chocolate, much of which had been rendered unusable by puncture holes and saliva. Then I surveyed my packs for other losses. As I made my rounds, I could see that portly fellow sitting in the woods intently watching my every move. And I quickened my pace. Sorting through one rifled pack, I found, much to my dismay, two loaves of bread, half my stock, had changed hands – or paws, if you will.

That made me mad. I turned and yelled again. And grabbing a rock from the ground, I threw it into the woods, driving that furry thief back farther still. I should add, I am no fool, so I made certain that the rock missed its supposed target by quite some distance. I saw no reason to unduly provoke an animal of his stature, one that surely would have done me irreparable harm in mortal combat.

When the bear had vanished from sight, I slid down the short slope into the woods and proceeded to gather pieces of bread from the forest floor. What moments earlier had been two loaves of bread was now a well worn one.

I placed my salvage in a sheared wrapping and climbed back up the rise. As I emerged from the trees, I discovered, adding further to my dismay, that the bear had circled around and was now standing smack dab in the middle of my camp. But my confidence as a chaser of bears had grown considerably since my first attempt, so I yelled again. It was my most imperious command of all. This time, however, his response was anything but compliant. Resolutely holding his ground, he issued a double woof, while jumping several inches off the ground.

I stumbled back. I am usually a slow learner, but this was one time I immediately grasped the significance of the exchange: my bear-chasing days were over, and I hoped that that was all that was ending. My heart sank to the tiniest crease in my water-wrinkled toes; and my thoughts raced to grizzly country in Glacier National Park, the gruesome tale of the killing of two girls and all of the attacks I had heard of since: attacks frequently harbingered by a foreboding series of woofs. I felt that my demise imminent and I silently made peace with my God and myself.

But no attack came. Regaining my composure for a second time, I began to talk, drop my tent and pack my gear in one nonchalant, fused motion motion. All that came to mind was spoken. I asked that bear how he could be such an inhospitable host to such a congenial guest like myself;

and what his parents would think of him if they could see his rude behavior now; and if he no sense of propriety or common decency; and how he would like some boorish bully to rifle his belongings without his permission. Yes, I asked that bear anything I could think of that might appeal to a bear's code of ethics, or even tweak a subconscious pang of Freudian guilt.

Throughout this rather lengthy, disjointed entreaty, the old boy just sat there with a quizzical look shrouding his face. Even a bearish smile, I may have detected; but then again, it was probably imagined. After all, I was grasping for the slightest relief from this most unnerving situation.

Still, I was fortunate. The bear stayed put, a perfect audience, studiously watching, as this long lanky creature babbled on and on. Finally, with everything ready for what I hoped to be a quick and uneventful departure, I turned my canoe, pushed it into the water, loaded my gear and paddled out on to the lake. About fifty yards from the shore, I looked back. My nemesis had wandered down to the water and was lounging lazily on the sandy beach. Now the way I figured it, as we eyed each other, this territory was his not mine. I was only borrowing it for a while, and if he didn't want me there, I sure didn't want to stay. Besides, given the situation, I thought that a draw was pretty darn acceptable. He got the camp, and I got my food – and, oh yes, an intact body too.

THE END

A CAMPFIRE STORY

The Strange Tale of John Decamp

My uncle Carl used to say, "If you can't tell a good story, there's something important about living that you've failed to grasp." In telling this tale, I would add, being in the right place at the right time helps immeasurably. Let me explain.

My friend Jim Rowley and I first heard about John Decamp in 1971. That year was the second summer we ran canoe trips for high school students to the Quetico-Superior wilderness in northeastern Minnesota and northwestern Ontario. Jim and I had staked out a couple of bar stools at Elna's, our favorite watering hole in the small, outfitting town of Ely, Minnesota. We were somewhere between our second and third beer when one of the bar's patrons approached us with a proposition.

"Boys," he said, "you look like you just got off the water. I'm not sure bein' out there on those lakes is such a good idea."

"How's that, partner?" Jim asked.

"Well, it's like this. For the price of a drink or two I'll tell you a story that will make you think twice before you settle into that canoe of yours for another trip."

Of course, we bit and have never regretted it.

The old man's story began nearly three hundred years ago. North American furs were high fashion in Europe and the demand seemed insatiable. By 1778, the year our raconteur's tale began, the fur trading business was highly competitive and dominated by one major player, the long established Hudson Bay Company, and several of independent traders operating mostly out of Montreal.

Trade in this vast continent's interior was conducted entirely by canoe. Large birch bark cargo canoes carrying trading goods and up to fourteen men traversed the northern regions of North America. From Montreal in the east to Great Slave Lake and the Mackenzie River in the *pays d'en haut* – the fur trader's term for the northwest – work was performed in the company's service. And the labor of this economic endeavor was transacted by the voyageur, a canoe man who took great pride in both the physical demands and the history of his chosen profession.

By the spring of 1778, trading activity in the interior had become so intense that experienced voyageurs were in short supply. Independent fur trading companies working out of Montreal were numerous, and many of them resorted to assembling blended crews of experienced and novice canoe men. Frequently, the novices were not the most savory members of this frontier society. Sometimes simply needing to leave town quickly explained their motivation for taking a job for which they were ill-prepared. The focus of this story is a company of canoe men that included three such individuals.

In late winter of 1778, Henri St. Claire was commissioned by an independent trading company to assemble a brigade of man and five forty foot Montreal canoes called *canot du maitre.* The brigade totaled 70 men in all, mostly experienced voyageurs. Among St. Claire's otherwise strong crew were three inexperienced fellows who had signed up as *hivernants*, a position that required an employee to spend the winter in the interior. This was unusual since the *hivernants* were normally made up of the most experienced voyageurs. The three men were Jacques LaRue, Connie Laframboise and Neville Courtland. Their pedigrees were questionable and each of them most likely had a good reason to leave Montreal quickly. Criminal charges, persistent creditors, or jilted husbands seeking reprisals – the reasons for their sudden departure were never made clear. But on the morning of April 15th, 1778, the three men were at their posts, learning, probably for the first time, to stroke their paddles quickly and in unison with the more experienced members of their party.

The canoes moved over the Great Lakes, making their entry into the interior at the nine-mile long Grand Portage on the Pigeon River at the western end of Lake Superior. St. Claire's brigade based its operation in what is today called the Quetico-Superior region. The heart of the area is a maze of nearly 2,000 interconnected lakes and is today protected as wilderness on both sides of the border. The area is vast, and, in 1778, it was full of fur bearing animals.

St. Claire had worked this area before and had developed a relationship with the native people of the region. Called Ojibwa, they lived for most of the year in family units scattered throughout the lakes. The families gathered twice a year in the spring and the fall, first to tap the maple sap and later to harvest the wild rice. The timing of the crew's arrival in the region was, therefore, vital. During the sap harvest St. Claire would negotiate the terms of trade for the coming year.

The negotiations typically took three days. The Ojibwa families would select a respected elder to represent them in these talks. That year, *Makoganj* was chosen for this duty. He had negotiated with St. Claire before, and the two men had established a trusting relationship.

Makoganj's family camp was on a large island on Saganagons Lake. During the negotiations, one member of the old man's family in particular received constant notice. She was the old man's granddaughter, *Minojaabi* – Ojibwa for beautiful eyes. She was the subject of many conversations around the winter fires back in Montreal, usually in a lustful tone. The men would describe her flawless beauty and how it would have surely rivaled that of the great legends from antiquity.

With negotiations concluded, the summer's toil began. The work was hard and continuous, and the days were long, sometimes lasting fifteen hours or more. LaRue, Laframboise, and Courtland soon realized that facing their fate in Montreal may have been the better choice. Although summer had been hard, winter promised to be unbearable. So the disgruntled canoe men hatched a plan. During the first three weeks of September, they had been working several lakes just north of Saganagons. They determined that if they deserted their post immediately, they could make it back to Montreal before winter set in. But before departing on the long trip home, these three rogues devised a prelude to their plan, one that would leave its mark on this region for years to come.

On a moonless night in late September, LaRue, Laframboise, and Courtland crept into *Makoganj's* family camp and kidnapped his granddaughter, *Minojaabi*. The three men had been without female companionship for far longer than they were normally accustomed, and they felt that their summer's constant labor had entitled them to a sampling of the canoe country's most coveted prize.

Their plan was simple and direct. They would take poor *Minojaabi* to an island on a remote lake that they had spotted earlier in the summer. There they would bivouac for several days while enjoying poor *Minojaabi's* company. When their sexual appetites had been satiated, they would abandon the girl and head for home.

Unfortunately, the three men's plan encountered a major hitch. Winter descended on the area early and with a ferocity and persistence not seen since. The three men found themselves in a bit of a predicament. They had been trapped by nature, and they were hardly prepared to endure the harsh winter. They also found that their Ojibwa prize was now a major liability. The Ojibwa would surely search for her and, if found, they would incur the unforgiving wrath of the entire nation. Needless to say, their prospects seemed dubious at best.

Makoganj faced a predicament of his own. When he discovered that his granddaughter was missing, he called for other families to aid in the search for her. But the continuous snow, intense cold, and almost instant ice in of the lakes stopped the effort instantly. *Makoganj* was left waiting for spring. And that was a long wait indeed.

Ice-out occurred on April 22nd. Amazingly, the three rogues and even *Minojaabi* had survived the winter. Suspecting that *Makoganj* would likely resume his search, LaRue, Laframboise, and Courtland wasted no time departing for Montreal. Before leaving, however, in order to hold *Minojaabi*, the three men constructed a crude cage from the trunks of young pine trees.

Three days later, *Makoganj* arrived at the site of his granddaughter's containment just as the sun was setting. As the old man stepped from his canoe, he could hear wailing coming from a shadowy figure at the peak of the island. As he approached, the source of the wailing became evident. Within the cage, he could see the hunched over body of his beloved granddaughter, rocking back and forth emitting sounds that would have frightened a banshee. A close inspection revealed that *Minojaabi* had aged a lifetime during her several months of captivity. But most disturbing to *Makoganj* was that his granddaughter's writhing incantations only increased whenever a male approached the cage. The implication was apparent. *Minojaabi* would not recover from the ordeal she had endured.

That night, angry and distraught, *Makoganj* raised his eyes to the full moon that lightened the darken sky and issued this promise:

"I swear upon the spirit of my father and all who have gone before that when our people are banished from this land, a curse will befall the *waabishkiiwed* for fifty years," said

Makoganj. And looking at his caged granddaughter, "This I promise you my beloved granddaughter."

It is said that *Minojabbi* lived for another fifty years, but never regained her sanity. Confined to this island that she could never bring herself to leave, she received supplies from Ojibwa families throughout her life. The provisions were brought at the dead of night and always during the darkness of a new moon.

For years the maps of the region included the name Mad Woman's Island. When the recreational potential of the region began to be fully appreciated, the cartographers quietly removed the name from their newer maps.

In 1933 America was in the grips of the worst economic depression in its history. The nation's unemployment rate had just reached twenty-five percent and bread lines could be found in every major America city. Things looked bad. But even in the worst of times, opportunities exist.

John Decamp was a young engineering student recently graduated from the University of Chicago. Decamp had graduated at the top of his class and, despite the country's broken economy, he had received three good job offers in his field by graduation day. For this young engineer, the Great Depression was only a headline in the daily newspaper.

As a young man, Decamp had travelled in the Quetico-Superior region with his father and grandfather. Listening to the older men tell their stories around a flickering campfire was one of the highlights of his young life. With a major decision to make, Decamp thought there no better place to sort through his options than in the calming simplicity of this pristine wilderness.

On May 31st Decamp loaded his camping gear and canoe at his parent's house in the recently developed Rosedale Park section of Detroit, Michigan. Journal entries found later revealed the childlike enthusiasm he was feeling as he anticipated his first ever solo trip. Decamp's planned route involved entering Canada on Carp Lake and traveling east on a series of lakes known as the Man Chain before circling back into the United States on Knife Lake. There, he would paddle south and east through a series of smaller lakes on the American side of the border, eventually exiting the wilderness on Moose Lake. He estimated that he would need twelve days to complete his trip. As it was, the trip may well have ended up being the longest that young Decamp would ever take.

By late June, Decamp's parents had not heard from their son. It was not like John to cause his mother undue concern, since she was a consummate worrier. Finally, on June 25th, John's father succumbed to his wife's prodding and contacted the U. S. Forest Service. The agency checked its records and discovered that Decamp had used the voluntary sign-in procedure, but had not yet signed out. The Forest Service official informed Mr. Decamp that it was not uncommon for canoeists to ignore the last part of its safety procedure. After all, they may have felt that they were off the water safely and checking in seemed pointless. Mr. Decamp agreed to wait through the coming weekend before make a formal search request.

The search began on July 7th. Using Decamps proposed route, the Forest Service flew over the lakes on the American side of the border that were most likely to hold a key to his disappearance. On the second day, John's camp was found on the large island at the west end of Kekekabic Lake. The camp seemed orderly, as if it were still in use. Everything was there except for Decamp's canoe and paddle.

Upon further investigation the Forest Service found that on the ninth day of Decamp's trip the border town of Ely, Minnesota had recorded a bizarre weather event. For three days a massive electrical storm hovered over the lakes northwest of the town. The residents later reported watching in amazement this unrelenting light show. In addition to the intensity of the storm, the fact that the lightning appeared to barely move from a single point made this event especially memorable.

No trace of Decamp himself was found; yet, the Forest Service officials investigating the disappearance concluded that the young man had been out on the lake when the storm began and his canoe likely capsized and he drowned. Decamp had apparently committed a common error made by overly confident canoeists. His had left his life jacket in camp.

The search team packed up Decamp's gear and headed in. Conveying sad news was part of the job. The Forest Service official assigned this unpleasant task, concluded his conversation with the Decamps with his condolence, and then asked them where they wanted their son's gear shipped. Mr. Decamp responded that he didn't care, but that he never wanted to see any of the items associated with this tragedy again. Ultimately, the camping gear was tagged and sent to a Forest Service warehouse outside of Duluth, Minnesota, where it sat collecting dust for the next fifteen years.

On June 22nd, 1948, the bodies of two canoeists were discovered washed ashore on White Island on Basswood Lake. At first glance it looked as if the men had drowned, but a closer inspection of the bodies revealed something suspicious. Both men had a circular indentation half the size of a dime in the middle of their forehead. It was enough to warrant an autopsy.

The forensic procedure was performed in Duluth. The medical examiner quickly concluded that both men had died instantly from blunt force trauma to the head. The skulls had been fractured and no water (requisite evidence of drowning) was found in their lungs. It was clearly a homicide. But why here? Why would someone go to the trouble of following his victims into the wilderness to settle a score that could have been handled more easily and with much less suspicion almost anywhere else? It was a valid question and a good man would be needed to propose an answer.

Noah Larson had moved to Ely, Minnesota sixteen years earlier to take the position of chief editor for the town's only newspaper, The Ely Miner. The paper's owner, Peter Schaeffer, did not have to do much persuading since jobs were scarce in 1932. Besides, the new editor liked to fish.

Larson quickly became an experienced traveler in the canoe country, and, as a result, he had developed a comprehensive knowledge of the history of the region. Over the years, the new editor had heard several versions of the abuse inflicted upon *Makoganj's* beautiful granddaughter. Each version, however, had concluded with a verbatim account the old man's vengeful curse.

The Decamp incident had been a big story in town because of both the odd nature of the storm and Decamp's promising future. The combination of that summer's murders and the Decamp and *Makoganj* stories set Larson to thinking. Could these events be linked somehow? He soon had a possible explanation. Larson knew, however, his explanation for the confluence of these the three events would not be received well in Ely. He decided to launch his own investigation before presenting his theory.

Larson's first stop was just down the road at the local Forest Service station. The Forest Service, over the years, had kept thorough records of injuries and deaths occurring in the canoe country. Similar records existed across the border in Canada's Quetico Provincial Park.

The newspaper man took two days assembling the data for which he was looking. What he discovered was troubling. The records clearly showed that beginning in July 1933, one or two people died in the canoe country every month between May and September. All of the incidents involved a single canoe traveling alone and all of the deaths had been attributed to drowning. Until June, no bodies had ever been found.

When Larson returned home he charted the lunar cycle using old calendars he kept in his study. Slowly a pattern emerged. Each of the missing canoeists' travel had overlapped a period of a full moon.

This coincidence piqued Larson's interest. The following day Noah called the Superior National Forest Headquarters in Duluth. He had conversations with several Forest Service employees before finding someone who remembered the Decamp incident. In fact, John Shirley not only remembered Decamp, he had headed the search team that had found the missing man's camp.

Larson asked Shirley about the condition of the camp, the efforts taken to find the body, and what had happened to Decamp's gear. On the last question, Larson hit pay dirt. Shirley informed him that the gear had been labeled and stored in a government warehouse outside of Duluth. So far as he knew, it was still there. Larson asked Shirley whether he thought the service would mind if he examined the equipment. Shirley responded that he could see no reason why it would be a problem.

Two days later, with his appointment set, Larson drove the hundred and twenty miles to the Forest Service warehouse. The warehouse caretaker, a man in his late sixties, and had managed the facility for nearly thirty years. The catalogue of its contents resided both exclusively and accurately in the old man's head.

"Decamp? Sure I know where the poor boy's stuff is," the caretaker quickly responded as they both walked down a long, dusty aisle.

And there it was, labeled and neatly stacked, just as Shirley had left it fifteen years earlier. Larson immediately began his examination. He untied and unfolded all of the gear, laying it out on the warehouse's concrete floor. Larson had no idea what he was looking for; he was just looking.

More than an hour passed while Larson scrutinized each item meticulously, but nothing appeared unusual or out of order. Disappointed, he repacked the gear and returned it to its shelves. He thanked the caretaker and headed north to Ely and home.

On his drive, Larson kept replaying the images of the gear in his head. As he approached Virginia, Minnesota, he suddenly realized that something wasn't right; something was missing from Decamp's gear.

"The grate, the cooking grate! Where was Decamp's grate?" Larson questioned. He quickly turned his car around and headed back to Duluth.

The caretaker was locking up when Larson returned. The two men talked briefly and the caretaker promptly reopened the door. Both men walked the aisle to the caretaker's office. The old man rummaged through a slightly disorganized file cabinet looking for the file containing the original inventory of Decamp's gear. With the file located, Noah carefully examined the list – a cooking grate was listed on the inventory. Larson asked if he could have a little more time and the caretaker consented. "Time's all I've got these days," the old man said with a chuckle.

Larson had an idea what had happened to the missing grate. The bottom portion of the shelf holding Decamp's gear included a set of sliding drawers. The drawers concealed anything that may have fallen between the shelf and the wall. And there it was, the missing grate wrapped in a soiled cloth sleeve. Noah removed the grate from its packing sleeve. At first glance, he found what he was looking for.

One tine had been broken from the grate. It was obvious that the tine's removal had occurred after the grate had been last used for cooking. The weld points that marked where the tine had been attached to the frame of the grate were shiny silver rather than blackened from countless fires. And most interestingly, the diameter of the tine was identical to the indentations in the skin of the two men found dead that summer on Basswood Lake.

Larson had an idea of where to look next. He and his wife Elizabeth had yet to take their annual summer trip. Larson suggested that Quebec might be a great destination. The old city, he explained to his wife, had all the charm of Europe before the war without the expense and hassle of getting there. Elizabeth agreed. Larson was pleased, for he had another reason for this seemingly romantic vacation.

Bibliothèque et Archives in Quebec City housed most of the administrative and judicial records from the fur trading period. What Larson hoped to find was a record of LaRue's, Laframboise's, and Courtland's employment by a fur trading company in 1778. What he actually found was even more intriguing. Larson discovered court records for the prosecution of three men in 1780. The charge: the lewd and lascivious molestation and carnal knowledge of a female member of the Ojibwa nation during the winter of 1778-79. For reasons known only to officials now long deceased, the records were incomplete and unusually vague. The names of the three men appeared nowhere in the record. The court, however, must have viewed this offense as a grave one since each of the men was sentenced to death and summarily executed.

Back in Ely, Larson began to talk about the summer murders. His explanation ran something like this. Fifteen years ago John Decamp had been launched as the instrument to fulfill *Makoganj's* prophetic curse. According to Larson, Decamp had not drowned during the three day lightening storm. He had been on his island camp when the storm began. The lightening seemed to the residents of Ely not to have moved because it hadn't. It had entrapped Decamp like the cage in which poor *Minojaabi* had been placed. In both cases the cages – one wooden and one electrical – had driven their respective prisoners mad. When the storm subsided, Decamp left the island with only his canoe, paddle, and the missing tine. For the past fifteen years, Decamp had been stalking canoeists and exacting *Makoganj's* revenge, always on the night of a full moon. The vengeance was both swift and symbolic, a fatal blow to the head with the missing tine. The mark of the full moon was thus permanently stamped on each victim's head, just as the memory of that full moon had been stamped on the old man's heart during the moment of his greatest sorrow and most intense rage.

Although an interesting explanation, it was not one that would be easily accepted by a community in the early stages of developing a recreational wilderness business. Larson got the message and promptly ceased pushing his "fanciful" yarn. And the story quietly died.

Well, Jim and I thought this was a pretty good story and one that was certainly worth the price of a couple of drinks. If nothing else, we thought, we could tell it on future canoe trips and scare the wits out of at least a few of our young campers. After all, what is a camping experience without a frightening, campfire story?

But then things began happening – To Us.

The summer following first hearing the Decamp story, we were guiding a trip in the American part of this canoe country wilderness. We were on a route that begins and ends on the Nina-Moose and Little Indian Sioux rivers off the Echo Trail. Our trip was in its third day, and we were camped on Pocket Lake. We had taken a layover day, and the kids had busied themselves with fishing, swimming, and general camp nonsense.

It was late in the afternoon when one our young campers, Jim Duggan, returned to camp after foraging for firewood. In addition to a stack of wood, Jim was carrying an old metal can. He had found the can embedded in the root of a pretty good size red pine. We have always encouraged good leave- no-trace practices, and frequently carried out more debris than we had carried in. We congratulated the young canoeist on his excellent land ethic, and we then inspected the can. The can was empty of its original contents, but when I shook it something rattled inside. At closer inspection, the top of the can appeared to have been removed and then replaced. Over the years rust had formed over the whole surface of the can, fusing the top to its base. With a little prying with my pocketknife, I was able to remove the top.

Inside the can was a piece of well-aged birch bark. On the smooth inner side of the bark was carved a cryptic message:

· JUST A BURNING MEMORY

Underneath the message were two letters: JD

Up to this point we had never told the John Decamp story to anyone. Jim and I looked at each other silently speculating on the other's thoughts. The exchange must have seemed strange because the kids, who had by now gathered around us, immediately asked what was wrong.

We, of course, lied and answered, "Nothing." Even then, we suspected that our terse response was not convincing.

That evening we told the story for the first time. The kids were riveted to every detail, and, as the story unfolded, the can's significance became apparent to everyone. Then, as if on cue in a theatrical drama, the heavens opened. With the final word of the story told, a massive bolt of lightning ignited, and then another, followed by another, and another, and another – a seemingly unending cacophony that reminded all of us of Nature's relentless power. Accompanying this spectacular light show was a torrent of rain, causing all of us to rush for the shelter of our tents. The thundering symphony lasted a good forty-five minutes. The bolts of lightening were so close and so powerful that each time one discharged its energy we felt as if someone had flicked on an overhead light in our tents.

Needless to say, we had many worried campers that night, more, I suspect, from the timing of the storm, than from storm itself. If the truth be told, there were two worried guides as well.

The next morning I picked up the rusty can and the birch bark scroll, and packed it out. I decided that I needed to conduct my own investigation when I returned home.

I had met a Minnesotan two years earlier who was associated with the state's historical society. I decided to get right to the point. When I finally got Dan Baker on the phone, I asked him if he had ever heard of a guy named John Decamp. He had. Baker told me that Noah Larson's speculation had been floating about the canoe country for years.

I asked Baker what he thought about the story.

He replied that he had never placed any stock in it. "After all," he said, "curses are the main staple of most effective camping stories." I agreed, but told him about the events that had occurred days earlier on Pocket Lake.

I could not measure the degree of Baker's interest over the phone. He asked if I had the can and birch bark. I told him that I did. Baker then suggested that I send the items to him. He would have a couple of forensic experts that he knew at the University take a look at them.

The following Monday, I mailed the items to Dan and left with my family for a back packing trip in Montana's Glacier National Park. The trip went well, and the rest of the summer passed all too quickly. My summer had been so busy that I hadn't thought much about my conversation with Dan Baker. I had thought it odd, though, that he had not gotten back to me with the forensic conclusions.

The evening before the new school year was to begin I gave Baker a call. I could immediately tell by the tone in this voice that something was amiss. Apparently there had been a fire in the area of the lab where the items had been stored. The birch bark was destroyed and the rusty can had been badly deformed. One thing, however, had been established before the fire had occurred. The can had a serial number stamped into it. Part of the coding sequence indicated the year the can was actually made. The can had been manufactured in 1932, one year prior to Decamp's disappearance.

Baker apologized for the unfortunate mishap and wished me good travels in the canoe country. At the time, I remember thinking, "Huh, this is an interesting way to leave things."

The next summer, I was leading a trip in the south central section of the Canadian portion of the wilderness, Quetico Provincial Park. We were paddling north on McIntyre Lake. It was noon and time for lunch. My canoe mate Janet Treadway and I were first to the lunch site on the large island at the north end of the lake. Janet climbed out of our canoe to inspect the site. As I sat in the stern of our canoe waiting, I saw that Janet, returning from her inspection, was carrying a couple of items: a fairly new Sierra cup and a mutilated cooking grate. The Sierra cup had been sitting in the shade and was half filled with warm coffee. Apparently, someone had left this spot recently and possibly in great haste. The initials JD were etched on the bottom of the cup.

Two summers later the drama continued. We were camped in the eastern part of the Quetico on McEwen Lake. It was late in the evening, probably past eleven. The new moon allowed the stars to be particularly spectacular. Several in our party were sitting with us on a granite shelf enjoying this celestial display, when we heard the sound of a paddle stroking the water from the darkness. From the canoe came a soft and eerie voice.

"Is this the Jenkins' party," it said.

"No," I replied.

"Oh," it said. And the ghostly figure paddled on, up the lake.

The next year, following our canoe trip, I was sitting in Vertin's on Sheridan Street in Ely, Minnesota eating a sandwich. I started talking to a fellow named Ken Lewis who had also just gotten off the water. We both had stories – mine involved an encounter with a bear while on a solo canoe trip and his recounted surviving a storm on Knife Lake. We laughed and commented on our mutual good fortune.

Then he added, "You know, something really strange happened a couple of years age on one of my trips."

Lewis proceeded to tell me a tale that closely paralleled our own encounters. He and his group had been on That Man Lake on the Canadian side of the wilderness. The firewood around their camp had been picked over, so two canoes had paddled back to a shoreline supply of wood that they had spotted on their trip up the lake. As they loaded their canoes with firewood, they heard a whistling sound coming from the woods. There was no question that the whistler was whistling a distinct melody.

"I have a friend who is a high school band director." Lewis recounted, "I remembered the tune and whistled it for him. He knew it right away,"

He went on to tell me that the song was *Heartaches*. The song had been released by the Ted Weems Band in 1933, the same year that Decamp went missing. His friend knew the song because he had played in a college quartet. Their group had performed *Heartaches* and had worked out their arrangement of the song from an old Ted Weems' recording.

When I got home from my canoe trip that summer, I went to the library and looked up the song. Initially, Weems hadn't liked the song so he had one of his performers, Elmo Tanner, whistle an accompaniment rather than sing the lyrics.

Further investigation revealed that both Tanner and Decamp had grown up in Detroit, Michigan and had attended Redford High School, although six years apart. Tanner graduated in 1923 and, at the time, Decamp attended one of Redford's feeder elementary schools. In high school Tanner had begun honing his whistling skill and first displayed it in the school's spring musical. Frequently, high schools in Detroit would perform segments of their stage productions for fifth and sixth grade elementary students as part of school district's cultural enrichment program. When he first heard Weems' recording, Decamp may have remembered Tanner's high school performance. Lewis' story may have been more than an interesting coincidence.

In 1982 we arrived early at our outfitter. My stepdaughter, Linda, was in her second summer of employment with our outfitter, Tom & Woods. As I climbed out of the van, I saw Linda hustling up the gravel parking lot. She beckoned me aside.

"You're not going to believe what just happened," she said. And without waiting for my response, Linda continued. "There was a family out on a trip last week. Apparently, their son had been under a psychologist's care. Maybe schizophrenic. It's not clear. Anyway, it was the family's last night out and they were camped up around U.S. Point on Basswood. They're all sitting around the fire when suddenly the boy jumps to his feet, yells something like, 'Enough? It's not enough,' and runs into the woods." Linda explained. She paused a moment and then added, almost as an afterthought, "They have been looking for him for three days and have found nothing."

"Was there a full moon?" I asked.

"You bet," she responded.

We just looked at each other. Although our thoughts remained private, I am pretty sure we were thinking the same thing.

Now the way I figure it, *Makoganj's* taste for vengeance had not been satisfied. By 1982 Decamp would have been an old man or maybe even dead. At any rate, the boy, then only eighteen, was the perfect instrument for *Makoganj's*, shall we say, continued presence in the canoe country.

Who knows? Maybe even for another fifty years.

Over the years, I have been asked by our young canoe-ists if I thought this story was true. Frankly, I don't know. I do know this; I always check my calendar before scheduling a trip into the canoe country. You'll never find me on those lakes during a full moon. After all, only a fool or a Greek is brazen enough to tempt the Gods.

THE END

…and so there ain't nothing more to write about, and I am rotten glad of it, because if I'd a knowed what a trouble it was to make a book I wouldn't a tackled it and I ain't agoing to no more – *Mark Twain*

ACKNOWLEDGEMENTS

I wish to express special appreciation to Linda Reynolds and David Hanks. Without their assistance this project would never have been completed.

I would like to thank my sister and brother-in-law – Judy Seger and Roy Basdisarian – for assisting me with a final reading of this manuscript.

Finally, I would like to thank my wife, Patricia Drake, for her encouragement and help with this project.

To my canoe mates George Dirner, Ken Lewis, Scott Popoff, Jim Rowley, Armond Spickell, Janet Treadway and Matt Turton. Our travels together over the years in the Quetico-Superior wilderness have been a highlight of life.

To the students at Centerville, Beavercreek and Bishop Alter High School in Dayton, Ohio; Anderson, St Xavier and Harrison High Schools in Cincinnati, Ohio; Mount Vernon and Groveton High Schools in Fairfax County, Virginia; Hilbert High School in Hilbert, Wisconsin, Thunderbird High School in Phoenix, Arizona and Westchester High School in Los Angeles, California. Your willingness to engage in a wilderness canoe trip has provided me with so many wonderful memories and a deep sense of satisfaction.

To everyone who fought the good fight to save this wilderness from development. Your vigilance allowed me to discover wilderness.

Edward Abbey, Wendell Berry, Edward Hoagland, Sigurd Olson and John McPhee helped shape the way I see nature and wilderness, and my responsibility to them.